# Mysterious
# San Juan Island

by

JOSEPH W. REIGEL

ILLUSTRATED WITH PHOTOGRAPHS

ORCAS ISLAND HISTORY PRESS

Eastsound, Wash.

2025

*Mysterious San Juan Island*

ISBN: 979-8-218-61439-3 (Softcover)

*Printed in the United States of America*

First Edition

# BOOKS BY JOSEPH W. REIGEL

## SHIPWRECKS OF THE SAN JUANS

A complete history of maritime disasters in the San Juan Islands, from the earliest schooners to the naval aircraft of World War II.

## UNUSUAL ORCAS ISLAND

A collection of strange accounts and bizarre history from the "Gem of the San Juans," including UFO encounters, sasquatch sightings, ghosts, and everything in-between.

# Contents

*They told stories of the great Northwest, that was like a mythologic region to me, of the Chinook Indians, and of the San Juan Island and the English officers . . . I found myself wondering if it had been a dream . . .*

**LaSALLE CORBELL PICKETT**

*He requires haunted woods, and the friendly presence of ghosts . . .*

**RUPERT BROOKE**

*After all, what is every man? A horde of ghosts—like a Chinese nest of boxes—oaks that were acorns that were oaks. Death lies beneath us, not in front—in our ancestors, back and back until . . .*

**WALTER de la MARE**

# *Introduction*

Prior to the last ice age, the San Juan Islands of today were mountain peaks that towered above a wide and meandering river delta. Strange and primordial creatures darted through alien forests, while the seas beyond steamed beneath the low red sun. Millions of years later, during the Pleistocene epoch, the mountains were covered over with glaciers that eroded and smoothed and littered the landscape with tremendous boulders. It was nearly twelve thousand years ago that these glaciers receded, the seas rose, and the weird valleys were flooded and made the home of monstrous whelks, sharks, and octopi—and other things that have not survived in the fossil record. Today, San Juan Islanders live on the summits of this ancient range—a decidedly "eldritch" place, as one local Lovecraft fan phrased it.

San Juan Island, the second largest of the archipelago, was first settled by humans around fourteen thousand years ago. The progenitors of the present-day Lummi and Mitchell Bay tribes were said to have emerged from a portal on diminutive Guss Island, in San Juan's Garrison Bay—at least according to tribal lore. European settlement began in the early 1850s, when the Hudson's Bay Company established a sizable farm and sheep ranch near the future American Camp. Valuable limestone was discovered soon after, and the population swelled with Indians of other tribes, Celts, Appalachian hill folk, East Asians, Native Hawaiians, and all manner of people who some would hold to be well-attuned with the "music of the stars." Hogwash aside, the island's folklore quickly developed into the rich tapestry we find today.

The sources for this work range from first-hand accounts to ancient newspapers found bundled in leaky attics. For the sake of privacy, certain interviewees—at their request, of course—have been assigned pseudonyms, denoted with an asterisk (*). Otherwise, the stories are true to their sources. Their truthfulness, as always, will be for the reader to decide.

# How the San Juans Came to Be

Spieden is a long, five-hundred-and-sixteen-acre island lying just off the northern shore of San Juan. Known for its distinctive semi-barren appearance, like a piece of eastern prairie excavated and flung over the Cascades with an enormous spade, Spieden has long been fodder for rumors and bizarre legends—but few can top its role in the ageless legends of Lummi lore.

In their 1917 historical treatise *Washington, West of the Cascades*, authors Hubert Hunt and Floyd C. Kaylor related a Lummi legend of unfathomable age—the creation myth of Mount Baker and the San Juans, as recorded from the tribespeople themselves. Hunt and Kaylor's retelling is reprinted below in full.

"In the Northwestern Cascades stands Mount Baker, the 'Bride of the Pacific,' always white-robed.

In the Lummi Indian tongue the mountain is called Kulshan—once an active volcano, it is now accounted extinct. Kulshan means 'shot at the extreme end or very point.' It is not now known how long the mountain has borne this name nor exactly why it was given but it is very certain that Kulshan has been Kulshan for many generations. One of the most [knowledgeable] of the Lummi Indians attributes the name to the fact that the mountain was once conical and that the peak itself was destroyed by volcanic eruptions and explosions. The summit is not now conical but a cup-like crater. The name Kulshan is applied to other things than the mountain—any object that is long, slim or tall becomes 'Kulshan' when shot at, struck and aff-ected at the end.

"In the olden days, so the old folks tell us, Kulshan was a fair and handsome youth who grew apace to man's estate and then espoused two wives. One of these wives fully equalled her husband in beauty—she was the favorite wife and her name was Duh-hwahk. She bore Kulshan three fine sons. The other wife was no match for Duh-hwahk in beauty but she was very amiable, very kind and very attractive in manner. This wife was named Whaht-kway. Eventually it came about that the kindness and consideration of Whaht-kway so completely won over her husband that she supplanted Duh-hwahk in the affections of Kulshan. This, of course, aroused furious fires of jealousy and resentment in the breast of Duh-hwahk, who constantly kept the entire household in dissension and strife by means of her temper and her jealousy.

"Finally Duh-hwahk resolved to regain Kulshan by artifice. Relying confidently on her beauty and on her former firm sway over her husband she conceived the plan of feigning to desert him. So, one day, when it happened that by chance she found Kulshan in amiable and mellow mood and more pliant to her purpose, she complained to him of the coldness and harshness with which she, Duh-hwahk, had been treated in the household, even more by Whaht-kway than by Kulshan. She assured her husband that she loved him but that the burden was more than even her great love for him could bear and that unless he soon changed these conditions she must leave him and take with her all of her possessions. Kulshan resolved to be master of his own household and without hesitation informed Duh-hwahk that she could go as soon as she chose and as far as she liked.

"Duh-hwahk was dumbfounded by this unexpected reply. She felt that she must make things appear to him in a more serious light. She felt confident of his love and sure that at the last Kulshan would relent. Indeed she could not believe that he would really permit her thus to desert him. Founding her faith in this imagination, she gathered up her possessions and made ready to go at once. She prepared her pack thoroughly, putting therein plentiful supplies of berries, fruit, sweet bulbs and even of beautiful flowering plants of many varieties. Thus amply provided with all that she desired she then said farewell and fared forth, leaving her three children behind. The children bewailed the going of their mother and with many lamentations besought her to remain. This greatly pleased Duh-hwahk at heart for she now felt assured of melting the indifference of Kulshan. She was sure that he would call her back before she had been able to go any very great distance. With this in mind she managed to set forth on a course that would take her the longest way. So also she traveled down the valley between the mountain ranges so as to be always in the sight of Kulshan as long as possible, thinking to give him ample opportunity to recall her.

"She had not gone far, however, before she realized her mistake and richly repented her hasty action. So, as she went along, she would ever and anon look anxiously back. Her heart surged tumultuously with a fond hoping and a vain longing to see Kulshan wildly signal for her return—how she hoped that he would do so! Alas, she had gone too far for that, perhaps, and, besides, many little hills and valleys now intervened between her and home where she had left Kulshan and the weeping children. Therefore she must climb the knolls and pick out the highest hills from which to gaze back with longing eyes and sinking heart. Standing on the very summits of these hills she would strain with all her might, up to the very tips of her toes, seeking some sign from her loved husband. Sometimes she fancied she was not quite high enough and she would raise to her tiptoes and stretch forth her head in anxious gaze, yearning all the while and striving all the while to be just a little taller.

"This oft-repeated wish and effort soon began to have its effect upon her and she forthwith began to grow taller. At last she had gone so far that she must of necessity make camp. She selected for her stopping place one that seemed most satisfactory to her because from it she could have a clear view of her dear home so foolishly and uselessly abandoned. Here she removed her packs and cast the contents broadcast, blessing the place with all the stores of fruit, of berries, bulbs, tubers and beautiful flowering plants of many wonderful varieties, all of which she had taken away from Kulshan. There, looking ever and longingly northward, Duh-hwahk remains to this day and you may see her if you wish—look to the south and east—it is Mount Rainier. Therefore we know why all these beautiful things abound about Mount Rainier where Duh-hwahk cast them forth before she herself became the mountain. To the north lies the deserted husband, Kulshan, robbed of fruits and the beautiful things which Duh-hwahk took with her. Look to the north and you will see him, but the white man calls him Mount Baker, not Kulshan! All about Kulshan too you may see the deserted and weeping children.

"In time the faithful Whaht-kway felt the premonitory pangs of childbirth. She yearned for the comfort and company of her people, and especially the advice and assistance of her old mother. None other than that old mother could give the needed care in the

7

hour of trial. Kulshan listened to the pleadings of his faithful wife and yielded to them. Full well he knew, however, that the journey would be a hard one for Whaht-kway if she had to climb the mountains and journey over all the intervening heights and valleys. Therefore Kulshan engaged all of the animals with paws, from the lion to the mouse, to dig a long ditch from his home down to tidewater. This was done until the flow of water from his place was at last sufficient to enable a good-sized canoe to float down in safety. This stream we now know as the Nooksack River—adown it softly floated the canoe of Whaht-kway in these olden days when the river itself was new.

"At last she reached her beloved Hwulch or Puget Sound, her own country. Down between the many islands the canoe made its way and in passing each of these islets Whaht-kway made sure to leave here and there certain edible things—where they may be found to this day. When Whaht-kway at last reached home her parents greeted her fondly and asked her what position she chose to assume. She remembered how the jealous Duh-hwahk had reared herself up, up, up into the air until she became a mountain peak. Whaht-kway would not do so. She chose to lie down so that coming people would be able to reach her head without great trouble or without climbing—with Duh-hwahk, alas, it is different. Whaht-kway is now an island low lying, to the north of San Juan Island. Whaht-kway is now better known by the name of Spieden

Island and just a little north of it is the baby island which was born after Whaht-kway reached this place. At present all of the small islands between Kulshan and Whaht-kway bear the names of fish or some of the other edible things that Whaht-kway placed there as she passed by on the journey home. Many have cause to this day to remember with gratitude the generous thoughtfulness of Whaht-kway.

"During all this time Kulshan was lonely indeed. Instead of having two wives he found himself with none. All the while he kept straining upward to see if he might not catch occasional glimpses of his departed wives. The children saw him and did likewise, profiting by the example of Kulshan. Today Kulshan and Duh-hwahk are mountains and the children are the mountains south and east of their father Kulshan. We have told you what the word Kulshan means— but what does Duh-hwahk mean? It means, and how fittingly, 'clear sky.' So too Whaht-kway means a maiden who has just reached womanhood.

"This is the story of Kulshan, his two wives and his many children, and of how they came to be what they are and where they are."

# American Camp

The children of the earliest settlers had found countless skeletons protruding from the crumbling banks of Cattle Point. The area around American Camp had been inhabited by Native peoples for over ten thousand years, and their dead were interred in shell middens along the bulk of the windswept promontory. These children were no archaeologists, however, and would often set up the remains on nearby fenceposts as targets for stone-throwing.

The land had been the center of the Pig War dispute. Adjacent to the future American military encampment was the old Belle Vue Farm, a Hudson's Bay Company post first established in 1845. In that year, the American and British governments had signed a treaty formalizing the 49th parallel as the international boundary. The treaty had defined the precise border as spanning "the middle of the channel between the mainland and Vancouver Island." Regrettably, no cartographers had been consulted in this decision, and the two governments took up distinctly divergent viewpoints: the British claimed the aforementioned strait to be Rosario, leaving the entirety of the San Juan Islands under colonial control. The Americans disagreed, contending it was *Haro* Strait. Chief Factor James Douglas, the head of the Hudson's Bay Company presence in Western Canada and a representative of the British government, dispatched an operative named Roderick Finlayson to San Juan in 1845, to install wooden markers establishing the island as a British possession. By 1851, however, the need for something more substantial to maintain their claims was becoming clear; and so the company dispatched men to build a physical outpost on the island.

Joseph McKay and the Scotsman William John MacDonald landed with four French Canadians and a contingent of Indian canoemen in June of 1851. The men built a primitive cedar bark structure on the shore of Eagle Cove that would serve as a base for their salmon saltery. Around the same time, a Hudson's Bay sheep ranch and produce farm was established under the name Belle Vue, sitting on the site of the present-day American Camp. All not was not immediately well at these remote outposts; wolves, once common on the island, stalked the men by night, and the salmon run was particularly poor during their first season. By 1853, the saltery and the farm had merged together, and more substantial structures were erected.

Belle Vue, or "beautiful view" in the French language, was named for its unrivaled panorama of Haro Strait, the Vancouver coastline, and the dull sawblade of the Olympics some forty miles distant. It had consisted of six squared-log cabins built on a courtyard overlooking the water. Eighty acres were cleared and fenced for oats, and beyond were the sheep's broad pasturelands that stretched far along the natural prairie. Over a thousand sheep were landed on the island in December of 1853, brought from the company's Fort Nisqually and herded ashore near the saltery at Cattle Point. MacDonald was replaced by a clerk named Charles J. Griffin, namesake of the near-by bay, who was deemed the more experienced man to spearhead the company's claims on the disputed island. He manned the farm with the help of several white employees and around fifteen Native Hawa-iians. The post, in the British government's view, would suffice to solidify their claim to the territory.

This landing of the sheep would have the opposite effect. The newly-appointed customs official in Port Townsend, Colonel Isaac N. Ebey, fired off a letter to the Secretary of the Treasury warning of the ever-encroaching British threat to the islands, writing: "Feeling fully convinced that they are ours under the treaty, I shall regard them as such until otherwise inst-ructed . . . and shall act accordingly with any foreign vessels seeking to trade among them." The landing of the "foreign sheep on American soil" was all that Ebey needed to act on his patriotic instinct. On May 2nd, 1854, he went to San Juan with four others and pitched his tent on Cape San Juan, with the intent of seizing the Hudson's Bay sheep as contraband. Griffin, deputized to arrest anyone disturbing the peace, responded in kind—a Hudson's Bay steamship was sent for, and Colonel Ebey planted the American flag on a ridge overlooking the farm. The buildup to the Pig War had begun.

Much occurred during the intervening years. The Territorial Legislature of Washington officially claimed the San Juan as an extension of Whatcom County, and in 1855 Sheriff Ellis Barnes went to the island with Edmund Clare Fitzhugh, William Cullen, and four others to once again attempt a seizure of the sheep. Billed as a "sheriff's auction," Barnes nailed up notices of a stock auction to cover the Hudson Bay Company's delinquent taxes. The men scoured the island for sheep, and finally located a pen of South Downs and Cheviot rams farther inland. After a brief confrontation with Griffin and his Hawaiian herders, in which revolvers were drawn, the Americans departed for Bellingham Bay with the sequestrated sheep in tow. They narrowly escaped a pursuing company steamship under cover of darkness.

Meanwhile, American settlers were pouring into the islands at an alarming rate—at least in British eyes. The Hudson's Bay Company was already losing its foothold in the area, as Fort Nisqually and Fort Vancouver were becoming increasingly encircled by American homesteaders, and the British had no intention of allowing this final outpost to fall.

Isaac Ebey was instructed to keep a representative posted on San Juan, a duty he assigned to customs officer Oscar Olney. Olney would only remain for a year, departing sometime after the Port Gamble incident of 1856, when sailors from the USS *Massachusetts* engaged a Stikine raiding party from southern Alaska. A fracas ensued, resulting in the deaths of twenty-six Stikine and a single seaman. The northern natives had returned the following year, eager to avenge their dead by taking the scalp of a *hyas tyee*—a powerful white chieftain. Olney fit the bill as a government agent, and after being warned of the coming war party he lost no time in leaving the isolated outpost. Soon after, the Stikine called on Ebey's Whidbey Island homestead and left the Colonel scalped on the windswept prairie south of Coupeville.

The next customs man posted to San Juan was Paul K. Hubbs, Jr., appointed in April of 1857. Hubbs, who would eventually become one of the archipelago's oldest and most notorious residents, was the well-educated son of a territorial politician. He soon made a name for himself, as he almost immediately complained to Major Granville O. Haller, the U.S. Army commander in Port Townsend, of the frequent Indian attacks on his cabin. These northern Indians were drawn to the area by the friendly trade policies of the British, said Hubbs, and had been harassing him nightly with sporadic musket fire. Hubbs placed the blame squarely on the "tolerant" Hudson's Bay Company for allowing this behavior. When Major Haller sent a patrol to investigate, the hostile Indians promptly scattered.

American survey officials finally arrived in June of 1857. With the Royal Navy's cooperation, a joint expedition was launched to conduct study of the islands and reach a compromise—whatever that would entail. Little came of it; while the British offered to cede the entirety of the islands east of San Juan, the Americans refused. San Juan Island was viewed by both sides as a highly strategic locale; a Gibraltar or "Kronstadt" of the Pacific Northwest, as it was sometimes called. Relations between the two nations were naturally not as friendly as they are today—only a few years later, during the Civil War, the British would actively assist the Confederacy with arms deals and military advisors. And around seventy years after that, in the years leading up to World War II, the Royal Canadian Air Force would conduct highly secretive photographic surveys of the San Juan Islands and nearby military installations. The purpose of this mission, revealed only in recent years, remains a mystery; though per-haps it was related to Defense Scheme No. 1, the Canadian military's "hypothetical" plan for a preemptive invasion of the United States.

The deadlocked dynamic would change abruptly in the spring of 1858. Gold had been discovered in the

Fraser River Canyon, and prospectors from every corner of the continent and beyond were now flocking to the region. Almost overnight, Victoria had transformed from a relative backwater to a sprawling and sordid metropolis to rival San Francisco—and with this change came the usual unseemly characters. While most crowded up-river to the goldfields, some lingered behind and settled in the disputed islands. One of these men was a twenty-seven-year-old Kentuckian named Lyman A. Cutlar. He took up with an Indian woman and settled about a mile north of Belle Vue Farm, on the present-day site of the Frazer Homestead Preserve. It was this red-blooded, though unassuming frontiersman who would change the course of American and British colonial history forever.

Not long after, Cutlar had sailed the forty miles to Dungeness and purchased a peck of seed potatoes, which he promptly planted in his three-quarters fenced garden. This open side of the fence would prove the start of the trouble. A hefty Berkshire boar, one of forty owned by the Hudson's Bay Company, found its way to the freshly-tilled field soon after and began rooting for the spuds. As Cutlar himself later explained in a deposition:

"For some time I have been greatly annoyed by one of the Hudson Bay company hogs (black Boar) entering my potato patch and destroying the crop. He was repeatedly driven off by myself back to the Hudson Bay Company premises—about 1 ½ miles—

and they were aware of this fact. On the morning of the 15th I was aroused by some person riding by on horseback and upon going out the door found it to be Jacob, a colored man, one of the Hudson Bay servants. I immediately glanced towards the potato patch and seen the company hog at his old game. I immediately became enraged at the independence of the Negro, knowing as he did my previous loss, and upon the impulse of the moment seazed [sic] my rifle and shot the hog. I then went immediately to Mr. Griffin [...] and offered to pay for the hog. Or as I had some hogs on the island I would give one in place of that, for the hog annoyed me very much.

"Then Mr. Griffin flew in a passion and said, 'it is no more than I expected, for you Americans are a nuisance on the island and you have no business here and I shall write to Mr. Douglas and have you removed.'

"Then I said to Mr. Griffin, 'That is not what I came here for. I came here to settle for shooting your hog.'

"Then Mr. Griffin said, 'The hog is worth one hundred dollars and if you choose to pay that, all right.'

"I said to him, 'I think there is a better chance for lightning to strike you than for you to get a hundred dollars for that hog.

"Then I left Mr. Griffin and returned to my house. This was in the morning. In the evening Mr. Dallas, Mr. Fraser, Dr. Tolmie, Mr. Griffin [...] and [Jacob] came to my place on horseback. They stopped in front of my house.

"Mr. Griffin said, 'Mr. Cutlar, we wish to speak with you.' I walked out and asked what they wished. Mr. Dallas said, 'Are you the man that shot that hog this morning?' I told him I was the man.

"Then Mr. Dallas said, 'If you do not wish to pay one hundred dollars for the hog we will take you to Victoria and see.'

"I then told Mr. Dallas, 'I do not think you will take me to Victoria if I know myself and I think I do.'

"Mr. Dallas then said, 'You had better be careful how you talk. The steamer is here and a posse of men. We can take you over with us'."

As it turned out, company official Alexander Dallas's threat was only a bluff—while a steamer had recently arrived, it was only a routine visit, and no armed lawmen were aboard. Cutlar remained on the island, though many, like early American settler Charles McKay, urged him to lay low.

"The gunboat came to arrest him and I had to plead with Cutlar to hide," recalled McKay, "for I knew Cutlar was a good shot and [he] was going to kill all that would come to arrest him. If there was any shooting to be done we all had to take a hand in it, for we could kill all that would come, for we were all fine riflemen. We could hit a 10-cent mark at 100 yards. So you see it was not fear that caused me to coax Cutlar to hide, but I did not want those men killed.

"So finally Cutlar took my advice and when they

came to arrest him they could not find him. That saved bloodshed. This is the story we told General Harney when we got the soldiers."

Brigadier General William S. Harney was the hardbitten career cavalryman who commanded U.S. military forces in the Pacific Northwest. A firm believer in Manifest Destiny, he quickly became involved in the San Juan boundary dispute. His views on the subject were perhaps the most extreme of anyone involved; for not only did Harney want the San Juans, but Vancouver Island, as well.

"The population of British Columbia is mostly American and foreigners; comparatively few from the British Isles emigrate to this region. The English cannot colonize successfully so near our people, they are too exacting. This, with pressing necessities of our commerce on this coast, will induce them to yield, eventually, Vancouver's Island to our Government. It is as important to the Pacific States as Cuba is to those on the Atlantic," wrote Harney.

That Fourth of July, the largest American flag that could be found was raised on a high promontory where it would be visible to all around—British and Americans alike—in a strong gesture of defiance against the Hudson's Bay Company and the British Crown. The island was awash with the "Spirit of '76," and the Americans, reared on tales of their forefathers' Revolutionary and War of 1812-exploits, seemed eager for a scrap. As McKay described,

"We prepared to celebrate the Fourth of July and

hoisted a fine flagpole and got a large American flag and had a glorious time. There were fourteen of us and we passed a resolution that each one of us had to make a speech. When it came time for the Welshman on the island to speak, he said we should not only be independent of Great Britain, but we should have a government of our own on such a beautiful island as this was. So we kept up our flag for four days.

"General Harney spied our flag with his glasses [from his steamer in Haro Strait] and told the captain to put the steamer in to the island to see what this flag means.

"General Harney said it was the first American flag ever hoisted on the island. Seeing such a strange thing as a man-o-war coming into our harbor, we all went to see him land.

" 'Are you Americans?'

" 'Yes, sir.'

" 'Is that your flag?'

" 'Yes, sir.'

" 'What are you doing here?'

"So we told him we were settlers. When we found out who he was we commenced to lay our complaints to him against the Hudson's Bay Company and the Indians. We asked him if he would send us a company of soldiers to protect us from the Hudson's Bay Company's threats to take us prisoners. They had sent a gunboat to take one of our men to Victoria, and we told him all about the hog scrape.

"The General said, 'If you will send me a petition

with twenty-five signers, I will send you a company of soldiers.'

"He left and we went straight to Bellingham where there was one company of soldiers."

The petition was sent on July 11th, 1859, and upon receipt General Harney sent orders to Captain George Pickett, commander of Fort Bellingham, to "establish your company on Belle Vue or San Juan Island." On July 27th, Pickett led the sixty-six-man Company D of the 9th Infantry Regiment aboard the USS *Massachusetts* at Bellingham Bay. In the foggy pre-dawn hours they disembarked at the Hudson's Bay Company's split-log dock at Griffin Bay, replete with horses and provisions and a few small artillery pieces. The site where they eventually garrisoned would become the famed American Camp.

By August, a total of four hundred and sixty-one U.S. troops had landed on the island, and the camp was formally named Camp Pickett. Buildings from the now-abandoned Fort Bellingham were dismantled and reassembled on San Juan, and work began on an extensive earthen redoubt overlooking Griffin Bay and the Strait of Juan de Fuca, overseen by 2nd Lieutenant Henry Martyn Robert—who would go on to write the enormously influential manual *Robert's Rules of Order*. The Americans made great headway in just a few years, and by 1862 the Hudson's Bay Company had abandoned Belle Vue Farm and returned to Vancouver Island. The Royal Mar-ines, meanwhile, settled into their cantonment on Garrison

Bay nearly ten miles to the north.

By that time, American Camp contained at least thirty-four structures and sat near a relatively new "boomtown" on Griffin Bay known as San Juan Town. George Pickett had slipped away to receive his famed general's commission in the Confederate Army, and with the joint-occupation decision of October 1859, the relations between American and British troops had eased into a comfortable camaraderie.

San Juan Town, or Old Town, was another matter. It began as five shanties and a pair of wells dug near the old Hudson's Bay dock on Griffin Bay, a short distance from American Camp. By many accounts, it wasn't such a bad place in the beginning—a small amount of gold had even been discovered. But eventually, reports began flowing in of "tent groggeries" and trafficked women in the little village, and San Juan Town soon enough earned its reputation as a rip-roaring and bloodsoaked frontier town. William J. Warren of the U.S. Boundary Commission visited the area in 1860 and recorded the following:

*There are about 20 houses, one of them is occupied by a storekeeper who keeps an exceedingly limited supply of goods, five or six are 'rum mills,' and the balance are vacant. The population of the place numbers about 30 or 40, the number being made up of [...] white men, Chinamen and Indians. Whiskey drinking seems to be the principal occupation. There were not more than half a dozen respectable Americans in the place.*

A nearby native encampment called the "Rancheria" provided Indian women to the American soldiers, and countless "whiskey sellers" imported illicit alcohol from across the strait. The military presence on San Juan had attracted the usual miscreants, all eager to profit off the infantrymen's loneliness and guaranteed pay. A special correspondent from a San Francisco newspaper called the *Daily Alta California* wrote extensively on daily life at American Camp:

*Adjacent to the headquarters there is a flagstaff with an American flag, and a six-pound brass field-piece at its base. Near is the office of the justice of the peace, and to the west, just beyond an Indian hut, is the barn from the yard of which the notorious Berkshire boar broke loose on his devastating and final raid on the potato patch of Mr. Cutler* [sic], *the hero of the "San Juan Imbroglio," which should in justice be termed the "Berkshire War."*

*From the north of the camp the road winds down the slope through the firs to the bay's edge. A short distance from the camp, in this direction, is located the 'Temple of the Muses' presided over by the Chapman Family. It is a round tent, not overly large, and nightly entertainments are given to the soldiers.*

*Camp life begins at 5 ½ o'clock—and the fifes, drums and trumpets keep up a general hubbub for nigh an hour. After breakfast, which is often just coffee and toast, there are drills, various labors, including guard duty, artillery experiments, cooks, carpenters, brick-layers and tailors, while others cut firewood.*

*The guardhouse inmates, of whom there were quite a number, have various menial duties such as cleaning the ground of stumps, by aid of oxen, cleaning up, or working at the trenches.*

*Dinner is at 1 ½ o'clock, there are various activities, at 4 o'clock everyone parades and the tattoo beats at 8 o'clock. Those with passes seek amusement in town—at the theatre, or elsewhere as their fancy leads them [...] A quick chat around the bright wood fire or a quick rubber of whist manages to kill time; and sleep to those not on duty soon leaves the camp to the solitude of the guard, only to be broken by the visits of Indian squaws, of whom quite a number are on the island. These, with liquor selling, are the only troubles which beset the officers, as both work perniciously on the men. Acts of ruffianism to the former, whilst under the influence of liquor, are not uncommon; but are severely punished. If liquor selling interferes with the discipline of the army, martial law will be proclaimed [...] at present the vicinity is free from another evil—gambling.*

Violence was simply a part of daily life at San Juan Town. Captain Lewis C. Hunt, camp commander from November of 1859 to April of 1860, wrote that "[...] Ever since knowledge of the joint occupancy, the desperadoes of all countries have fought hither. It has become a depot for murderers, robbers, whiskey sellers–in a word all refugees from justice. Openly and boldly they've come and there's no civil law over them. All the Indian tribes in the neighborhood— Lummi, Swinomish, the Skagit and even the Cowichan and the Victoria Indians flock here in quantities to supply themselves with poisonous whiskey. As a result, this is a perfect bedlam day and night."

Captain Hunt and his successors worked closely with the Royal Marine officers to quell such crime, but their efforts were often fruitless. In May of 1860, an Indian was gunned down by Bill Andrews in the muddy street and left overnight, surrounded by wailing relatives who were dispersed by an Army patrol the next morning. In 1863, a drunken dispute at Lyman Cutlar's cabin resulted in William Gibson murdering Thomas Wheeler with a carving knife. An unknown number of killings among the Indians also occurred, the bodies buried deep in the woods where no evidence would ever surface. Such was life at San Juan Town.

By the latter half of the 1860s, however, the days of lawlessness had largely come to an end. More stringent discipline was enforced at American Camp under the new commander, Captain Thomas Grey, and a few key-troublemakers—namely, the whiskey sellers Isaac Higgins, J.S. Bowker, and E.T. Hamblett—were run out of town. Augustin Hibbard, the lime kiln owner and notorious liquor dealer who had once harbored the fugitive Bill Andrews, was conveniently murdered by Charles Watts at Lime Kiln Point in 1869. Captain Grey would banish a total of fourteen "vagabonds" during his tenure.

The resolution of the boundary dispute in 1872 spelled the true end for both American Camp and the vice-ridden settlement it supported. A Port Townsend merchant named Israel Katz had opened a general store at San Juan Town just a year before, selling everything from dry goods to furniture to ship chandlery. The shrewd Katz no doubt expected the old town to remain the hub of island activity—but he was wrong. In 1873, San Juan County was officially formed, and the new county seat was established at Friday Harbor; a deeper port, and with a freshwater spring to boot. Katz was quick to abandon the dying town, and had soon enough moved operations to Argyle, a bustling village a few miles to the north. Later, when Argyle, too, began to fade, he moved again to Friday Harbor, where he opened the "Produce Exchange." Katz continued to operate an expansive farm at the old San Juan Town for years after—he had also made a small fortune as a moneylender, allowing him to purchase many local properties for pennies on the dollar. As Orcas Island pioneer James F. Tulloch wrote,

[Katz's] *policy was to get his customers started drinking by generously treating them to his vile liquor when they arrived. Then, when they were half drunk, selling them far more than they intended to buy. Then when settling-up time came in the fall and they were unable to pay, he always said "That's all right. Just give me a little note and let it run."*

*As soon as they acquired title to their lands he got them to secure their notes by mortgage, saying that "it was a mere matter of form. You know Katz will never crowd you." The natural result was that Katz soon became a large landowner.*

Though his Old Town mercantile had gone under, his produce farm was still in excellent form; at least until the Fourth of July of 1890.

On that day, while the Cattle Point-area settlers celebrated at Grove Hall with food, footraces, and fireworks, an elderly caretaker named "Whispering Pete" Seery was burning grass on the Katz farm. Katz had purchased Seery's farm some years before and retained the old man as a farmhand. It was a dry summer day, and the fire quickly spread out of control, raging over the fields until it reached the remains of San Juan Town. The long-abandoned buildings erupted in flame and soon there was nothing left of the wicked place save for a few cellar holes and stone foundations and melted whiskey bottles.

Katz was a wealthy man and likely little affected by the fire. He went on to serve as the Mayor of Port Townsend, becoming one of the first Jewish mayors in the Western United States. After a bizarre series of events involving personal tragedies, affairs, and a fatal dose of turtle oil, he vanished without a trace in January of 1917.

American Camp, too, did not fare long. The Americans held on for another two years after the British departure, but soon the order was given for troops to withdraw to the mainland. The land was opened for settlement by the U.S. General Land Office, with the exception of a six hundred-and-forty-acre parcel to the east of the old camp that was reserved for military use. American Camp, and the old Belle Vue Farm, was immediately homesteaded by Robert Firth, who had been the last manager of the Hudson's Bay property. Firth had given up his British citizenship to stay on the island.

A number of American soldiers had stayed on, as well: there was Christopher Rosler to the northwest, and George Jakle near his namesake lagoon. Jakle's wife had once been married to another soldier named James Bryant, who had settled on the timbered north end of Mount Finlayson. In the late 1860s, Bryant had brought his Irish-born wife Eliza to the site, along with their two-year-old son Frank. One day, Bryant had gone out duck-hunting near the future Jakle's Lagoon, on the shore of San Juan Channel. He grabbed his shotgun and kissed his pregnant wife goodbye and she returned to her ironing.

Eliza had a "premonition," however—an overwhelming sense that something terrible had happened to James. She grabbed little Frank and rushed down to the lagoon, only to find her husband drifting along comfortably astride a log. Relieved, she waved and called out and held up little Frank to wave as well—but when James waved back, his weight shifted enough that the log rolled over and he slipped into the icy black water. To Eliza's horror, he failed to resurface.

Perhaps believing she would find no one to help her at sordid San Juan Town, only a half mile up the beach, Eliza supposedly ran the full extra mile to American Camp for aid—little Frank was left on the beach with only a warning to "stay there." When she returned with a group of soldiers, there was still no trace of James Bryant; and her son was now gone, as well. Thankfully, the boy was later found to have wandered home and fallen asleep in the family's chicken coop. Still, the trauma of that day would take its toll, and Eliza lost her unborn child soon after. Her next husband, German-born George Jakle, would become the namesake of the fateful lagoon.

Ghastly incidents around American Camp were not limited to the 19th century. Shocking violence seemed to haunt the place like a curse, as evidenced by the murder-suicide that took place just off Cattle Point Road, near the old Rosler place and Cutlar's homestead, in April of 1987.

Sixty-six-year-old Marion "Pappy" Liles—a retired Navy veteran who had most recently worked as a school janitor—was on the outs with his wife, Patsy. The year before, they had moved from Oak Harbor to a trailer adjoining that of Patsy's son, Ronald Howard, and his family.

"Information was obtained indicating that domestic problems existed between Mr. Liles and his wife . . . and that these problems had worsened considerably over the last week," said Sheriff Bill Cumming. "Only the family involved knows what these problems are."

On the night of April 2nd, at around nine p.m., Pappy finally snapped. For reasons unknown, he grabbed his pistol and shot Patsy three times. No one was home next door to hear the reports.

Howard's son returned home around forty-five minutes later, followed shortly after by his father. Howard's nephew, who was staying with the family on a temporary basis, arrived at 11:45. His wife was off-island on a business trip.

Pappy Liles knocked on the door a few minutes after midnight.

"Ron, turn on the light and open the door, there is something wrong with Patricia," he called out from the dark.

Ron Howard flipped on the porchlight and opened the door, and his father-in-law shot him in the stomach. Before collapsing, he managed to knock the pistol out of Pappy's hand and lock the door—very likely saving the lives of his son and nephew. Pappy, meanwhile, returned to his trailer, entered the bedroom where his wife lay, and turned the gun on himself.

"It's worse in a small community," said Friday Harbor Mayor Jim Cahail. "More people know each other. You hope that this type of thing happens only in big cities. It does kind of hurt when it comes to your own community."

As for American Camp, the area officially became a part of the San Juan Island National Historical Park in 1966. It was a long time coming; the open grasslands were overrun with non-native rabbits, and hare-hunters had been causing mayhem for the past few decades. "The three monuments in the park were pock-marked and chipped and the inscription plates had been bruised by bullets," wrote historian Lucile S. McDonald, referring to the stone historical markers erected in 1904. With the advent of the park, the preservation of both American and English Camps would be ensured forever.

Grant Pilcher spent over a thousand volunteer hours at American Camp in the early 2000s, and his stories reflect a different, considerably spookier side of the present-day park. Sixteen U.S. soldiers had died of various causes ranging from disease to suicide—four from "unknown" causes in the final years of occupation, with one even being "carried off" by a pair of Indians from the Kanaka Bay village, never to be seen again. Loneliness, low pay, and alcoholism had wreaked havoc on the men's morale, filling a decayed and wind-whipped cemetery on the broad prairie bel-ow Robert's Redoubt. Though the remains there were supposedly reinterred at Port Town-send in the early 1870s, Pilcher isn't so sure.

"That area by the Redoubt always gave me the heebie-jeebies," says Pilcher. "It was a big fortification dug out for the artillery in the first year they were there, but they never used it, not even for practice. They decided that neither side should have any big guns like that on the island. So they ended up putting the camp cemetery down there. I think there were fourteen graves by the time [the Army] left, and, at least on paper, those graves were dug up and moved to a military cemetery in Port Townsend. But who knows if they really moved them [...] I'm sure it would have been a lot easier just to say that had, than to deal with, you know, corpses and skeletons and rotted-out caskets. So I'm not sure. I experienced a lot of really strange stuff down that way, which kind of leads me to believe that maybe not all of the bodies were moved.

"I was out at the Redoubt once, or below it, where the cemetery was, checking on some marble butterfly enclosures that someone had said the deer had gotten into. It was getting dark, and it was probably too late for me to be out there anyway [...] well, as I was heading back to the trail, I [suddenly] got this just awful feeling out of nowhere. An empty feeling, like total despair, I would call it. It just hit me like a ton of bricks. I had to actually stop and collect myself a little bit [...] and then, out of the corner of my eye, I saw a light. I looked up, and there was a lantern far away down the prairie, waving back and forth in the dark like someone walking. And this wasn't a flashlight, this was some kind of kerosene or oil lantern, without a doubt [...] that was pretty strange by itself, but the more I studied it, I realized whoever was carrying the light was coming towards me. The sun was down too, by this point, and all I could see was this big, tall shadow walking towards me with kind of a crazy [gait], swinging the lantern back and forth [...] every ounce of me told me to skedaddle, and I did. I didn't run, but I'd look behind me once in a while, and I'd see the lantern man still following me, and looking a little closer every time, so [...] I was the most relieved I've ever been when I got back to the car."

Pilcher also described strange, putrid smells that seemingly manifested at random, and blood-curdling screams coming from the woods around Mount Finlayson—along with the appearance of strange, ghostly, non-lantern lights.

"Yeah, I saw lights, but not at the cemetery. Another ranger actually saw little balls of light near the Redoubt. Again, not flashlights, and no human shadows or anything, either. I saw lights down by Fish Creek a few years ago, which isn't part of the Historical Park. I was there pretty early before dawn because me and my buddy were going out to the Salmon Banks on his little Boston Whaler he had down there. Anyway, I got there probably earlier than I needed to be, and I saw these lights moving through the trees while I was waiting in my car. I thought it was flashlights at first, but then I saw it wasn't. It was these little balls of light, kind of floating around like fireflies or something. But they were way too big to be anything like that. I've always wondered about that. My uncle told me there used to be a lot of weird old Indian ruins down there, before they put the houses in, but I don't know."

There had indeed been "Indian ruins" near the Cape San Juan marina. There had been large "concentric circle rosettes" made of stone along the future community beach, perhaps built by the same mysterious folk who had terraced the hills at English

Camp in more ancient days. In the 1970s, these ruins were covered over with rubble from a nearby housing development.

More physically-formed apparitions have also been sighted, according to park employees. Ran-ger Cindy Norris* had a few unnatural encounters to report:

"A common sighting around here is generally a soldier in full Pig War-era uniform," says Cindy. "It's nothing I've seen, but I do know someone who claims that she saw this soldier on a dark night not far from [the visitor center], on Cattle Point Road. He was transparent and sort of misty-looking. As a matter of fact, she drove right through him—and all she felt was a rush of cold air.

"We've also had reports of a woman who people have seen in the Officer's Quarters. I think maybe it's the spirit of Major Harvey Allen's wife, Mary, who lived there until 1868. She was a fairly prolific diarist, and we once found that a single light over an exhibit on her life had been turned on in the middle of the night, and no one could explain it.

"I think the strangest, for me, is that people will claim to see wolves, sometimes. I've had a person from out of town tell me that they saw a wolf, or an absolutely huge dog, crossing the road not far from the lighthouse. Like a coyote, only about six feet long. There had been grey wolves on the island at one time, but they were wiped out by the farmers and Hudson's Bay people in the 1860s [...] so, when I hear that someone's seen a 'huge dog' or a wolf, I have to wonder if what they saw was really *alive* or not."

Closer to the old San Juan townsite, similarly supernatural stories have surfaced of a malignant atmosphere and unexplainable phenomena. Though traces of the old buildings have long vanished, the historically-minded visitor will find it easy to envision the roughhewn barrooms and butcheries that once crowded below the high bank and sloughed their evil discharge into the rusty saltgrass of Old Town Lagoon; it was here that artist Angie Kress had a rather unnerving experience in the late 1990s.

"It was unforgettable. I'd spend a lot of time around Cattle Point when I was living on San Juan, usually around sunset or in the early morning for my plein-air watercolors. One morning, I hiked down to the beach to do a little painting at the lagoon. I think I'd meant to go to Jakle's but I decided to stop at the Old Town Lagoon instead, just because it was so beautiful that morning, with the mist floating over the water and the pink sky […] like it's already a masterpiece. I set up my easel on a little rise where I had a very nice view looking over the lagoon and all the way up to Jackson's Beach [...] and, all of a sudden, I got this strange feeling that I was being watched by two people, or beings [...] I remember very clearly thinking, 'there are two sets of eyes watching me right now.' But there was no fear or anything like it—it was almost a calm feeling. And, when I turned around, there was a Native American man who was shirtless and wearing these beaded buckskin leggings, standing about twenty feet behind me on the meadow [...] and next to him was a huge wolf, both of them standing perfectly still. The power that I felt was so raw that I felt totally frozen, or not able to move at all. I made eye contact with this man, who I sensed was a warrior, and we held it for a few seconds [...] and then he and the wolf just gently faded away into the air, like a distant memory or a dream. I was so moved that I stayed and did complete my painting, and I included the two spirits in the painting just as I had seen them. Ever since then, I've felt as though they've been my protectors. I keep the painting in my studio, and it gives me a great sense of inner peace and inspiration. I wouldn't sell it for any amount of money in the world."

Do wolf spirits wander the windswept prairies of American Camp? Or ghostly soldiers from a forgotten graveyard, for that matter? There may very well be answers to such questions, but they won't be found in any guidebook or visitor center. Those inquisitive souls will have to hike the old trails to overgrown homesteads and ancient earthworks to find their answer, and even then it will likely not be certain.

# English Camp

When the first company of Royal Marines landed at lonely Garrison Bay in March of 1860, they found a weird and wild landscape unlike anything the Englishmen had ever seen; though the mysterious stone monoliths, reminiscent of the standing stones found in the remotest regions of Northern Europe, perhaps reminded some of their faraway home.

William J. Warren and Dr. Caleb Kennerly, operatives of the U.S. Boundary Commission, gave a detailed account of the bay as it appeared just prior to British settlement. The pair had been sent to covertly map the islands in January of 1860, to better aid the federal government in understanding the subtleties of the Pig War dispute; neither side, naturally, was satisfied with the idea of joint-occupation. Warren wrote of Garrison Bay:

*We camped on the site of an old Indian Village on the shore of a deep inlet or bay opposite the lower end of Henry Island. Portions of the old lodge were still remaining. It had been about 500 or 600 feet in length, by about 50 or 60 feet in width, and must have accommodated over a thousand Indians. As usual at such localities, there were immense quantities of clam shells on the shore.*

*Dr. K. and I climbed up a hill about 400 or 500 feet high* [Young Hill]. *From this eminence we had a very extensive view. To the south and west is a beautiful valley, mostly of prairie land. At the northeastern base of the mountains is a lake about ¾ mile in length and about 200 yards wide: its outlet is through a swamp into the north end of the bay on which we camped. A high bluff quite heavily timbered lies at the east. The valley south of us affords excellent grazing and has been used for that purpose by the Hudson's Bay Co . . . There are but few trees (oaks) scattered on the southern grassy slope of the mountain: the northern slope is covered with open timber, very much resembling the eastern slopes of the Cascade Mountains near the 49th parallel—the ground being free of underbrush and the grazing good.*

*On the hills we saw in different places cobble stones placed in lines about 100 feet long, arranged in this position probably by Indians . . . though for what purpose we could not conjecture.*

Other strange formations existed on little Guss Island, just five hundred feet offshore. Here, a circle of stones extended twelve feet across, with a tall monolith in the center—a place of nameless rites amid the bleached bones of the countless Indians interred there. The surveyors had stumbled across the remains of *Pe'pi'ow'elh*, a nine-thousand-year-old trading village, and the supposed emergence point of the first human on earth.

"The first man, *swet'an*, came down from Heaven to a place on the north end of our island. It was the center of the universe. This man became the ancestor of the *kale'gamis* people," said the Lummi Tribe—the *kale'gamis* being the progenitors of the Lummi, Saanich, and Songish peoples. Before the Moon of the Snow-Faced Men, the Lummi had controlled Garrison and Westcott Bays, the Songees had claimed the west side of San Juan, and the Saanich lived on the northeastern shore. Guss Island, once known as Deadman's Island, had been the first man's "point of origin into this world," according to state archaeologists.

For the Straits Salish, a people without a written language, time was marked by an oral calendar. Instead of years, or seasons, there were "Moons." A drought would be remembered as "The Moon of Dry Creeks," a wildfire as "The Moon of Great Fires." 1792 was the Moon of the Snow-Faced Men. It was the year that Captain George Vancouver arrived in the San Juans along with the Spaniards Quadra, Valdés, and Galiano; and it would mark the final "Moon" of the ancient village at Garrison Bay, which withered away until men like Warren and Kennerly found its ruins.

The land at Garrison Bay, though ideal in many ways, was considered bizarre and heathen by the Englishmen who first laid eyes on it. When it was finally decided that the Royal Marines would make their camp there, one naval lieutenant wrote, "I cannot help thinking this is a mistake after saying we would not send troops there for the last 9 months, that it was not 'English' [...]." Indeed, Garrison Bay had only been selected after more suitable locales near Cattle Point had been dismissed, due to their close proximity to the American camp. The colonial authorities desired a comfortable gap between the two factions, and so Marines were fated to make their cantonment among the weird stones and crumbling terraces below Young Hill.

The Marines at English Camp were a rough-and-tumble lot, culled from the combat-hardened Light Infantry battalions who had fought in the Second Opium War. Designated as "supernumeraries," or men without a formal unit, the volunteers had been lured to the remote Northwestern colonies with promises of extra "colonial pay"—assurances that were initially reneged upon by the local authorities. On the verge of returning to their respective units, their stay in British Columbia was soon necessitated by Lyman Cutlar's killing of the Berkshire boar in 1859, which precipitated the famed Pig War. The Marines were garrisoned aboard the frigate HMS *Tribune*, which rode at anchor in Griffin Bay until the initial hostilities had cooled. They returned to the Royal Navy base at Esquimalt, but by the following year had been assigned again to San Juan, this time after the joint-occupancy agreement had been reached with the Americans. They would remain at Garrison Bay for the next twelve years.

The contingent, consisting of eighty-three enlisted men and two subalterns under the command of Captain George Bazalgette, put ashore on March 23rd, 1860. Colour Sergeant Walter Joy, a senior enlisted man and veteran of the Crimean and Chinese conflicts, wrote of his initial impressions:

"Landed in a bay completely land-locked, our Camping Ground being on a shell bank—the accumulation of Years, evidently, as it averaged ten feet high, from thirty-five to forty feet through, by 120 yards long. It was the work of Indians, as they live very much on a shellfish called 'Clams', and of course deposit the shells just outside their huts, hence the bank I mentioned."

The exact cause of the abandonment of *Pe'pi'ow'ehl* was never truly determined; some speculated that the inhabitants had fled to Vancouver Island months before the Marines' arrival; others, that they had been driven away or massacred by the fearsome northern tribes, like the Haida or Stikine or Kwakiutl, who came to trade at the Hudson's Bay post in Victoria. Regardless, the village was now utterly deserted, and the Marines now set about leveling the middens and clearing out brush and trees. Barracks were erected along the beach, facing the water and bordering the expansive parade ground, while the officers were quartered high above in trim little houses on the oddly-terraced Young Hill. The iconic blockhouse was also built, serving simultaneously as a redoubt and as a stockade for errant Marines. Meanwhile, the ancient long-house, built of rot-resistant cedar, was partially recycled into the new construction.

By October of 1860, English Camp was a far different place. Gone were the mountainous middens and the massive and weather-stained longhouse; an early visitor, the Anglican bishop George Hills, described the cantonment as "picturesque and serene," and was impressed with the quality of the camp's vegetable garden.

Not all was "serene" at English Camp, however, or on San Juan as a whole. Whiskey-fueled violence was commonplace, and unscrupulous "vagabonds" did what they could to profit off the British and American garrisons; many American settlers, too, resented British claims to the vast and largely untapped limestone deposits at Roche Harbor, which the Marines occasionally quarried and burned for themselves. Bill Andrews was archetypal for the time; a laborer at the San Juan Lime Company kiln at Lime Kiln Point, he was accused of murdering two Indians, one of them near English Camp in 1863. Islanders penned a letter to Captain Bazalgette requesting intervention, as Andrews had so-far suffered no consequences. Bazalgette, in turn, wrote to his American counterpart, Captain Lyman Bissell, and suggested a jointly-led patrol to seek out witnesses and find Andrews. This was accepted, the patrol set out with several witnesses and soon tracked the murderer to Lime Kiln Point. However, it was soon discovered that Augustin Hibbard, owner of the kiln and a personal enemy of both Bissell and Bazalgette, was operating a sizable illicit whiskey ring. Andrews, having escaped the limelight, was given twenty-four hours to leave the island in lieu of a more fitting sentence. The names of his victims have been lost to time.

The little cemetery on a knoll of Young Hill tells a tale of its own. As historian Lucile S. McDonald described, "I climbed the stile over the picket fence and entered the enclosure to read inscriptions on five stones and a weathered cedar headboard. They dated from 1863 to 1865, and all but one were on graves of members of Her Royal Majesty's Light Infantry. The exception was William Taylor, the civilian storekeeper, who was shot accidentally by his brother. The longest read: 'Privats Jos. Ellis and Thos. Kiddy, who whare drowned Jany. 4th, 1863. This Tabblet is erected by their comrads. In the midst of Life we are in death'." In total, eight men met their end at English Camp during the military occupancy: three died of natural causes, four were drowned, and one was shot.

By 1872 the Marine garrison had dwindled below the required one hundred men, with the Admiralty noting that "some difficulty is experienced in [correcting] this at times without distressing the

Squadron." The San Juan outpost, though pleasantly maintained, had become some-thing of a backwater; and there was no undue controversy when the issue was finally arbitrated in the Americans' favor. The dilemma had been submitted to the newly-formed German Empire, and a three-man committee under Kaiser Wilhelm I ruled that the international boundary would span the center of Haro Strait. The British accepted the ruling and began returning troops to British territory. It was the last British territory ceded to the United States, and Governor James Douglas, the colonial administrator of British Columbia, wrote mournfully: "The island of San Juan is gone at last. I cannot trust myself to speak of it and will be silent."

The next occupants of English Camp were the William Crook family, who claimed the land under the Homestead Act in 1876. The family had arrived from Wyoming via covered wagon, and quickly converted one of the old barracks buildings into a home. The structure burned after a decade or so, and the Crooks moved into an officer's cottage on the hill—which itself burned some years later. Jim Crook, William's son, built a house by the parade ground in 1903, where he and his sisters lived for nearly seventy years.

Lucile S. McDonald visited the dilapidated camp a number of times, and described a rather unusual scene; elderly folk living amongst the decayed ruins like the last holdouts of a ghost town.

"On a cruise in the 1940s I first saw the blockhouse and remains of the encampment," wrote

McDonald. "James Crook guided us around and his sister, Mary Crook Davis, showed us a picture of the original camp. In a friendly manner she told us of her childhood there and how Indian women used to visit the bay 'to call their dead' from canoes."

Indeed, the Lummi hadn't forgotten their sacred connection to Garrison Bay and Guss Island. For many years, skeletal remains could be seen bristling from the eroded banks of the little island, falling into the sea and tempting the more morbidly-minded souvenir hunters of the era. For the Crook family, the discovery of Indian artifacts was no more remarkable than a farmer plowing up a fieldstone. "[Mary Crook Davis] thought nothing of using an ancient stone mortar as a door stop," said McDonald. More shocking, perhaps, was William Crook's burning of the little island, simply because he had grown tired of the "chanting" of Indian women who came to visit the dead.

"When I next interviewed the Crook descendants," she continued, "the visit was unlike my earlier experience. A number of years had passed and the pair had become eccentric in old age. Mrs. Davis was in a crotchety mood and Jim was occupied with a slingshot, using it to scare his bull away from the orchard. Jim looked like a trapper by then, wearing a visored homespun hat of his own weaving. The brother and sister clung desperately to their old fort and its surroundings, rejecting all efforts to purchase it for a state park. They earned a few dollars allowing visitors to walk around the grounds.

"Jim would show his relics in the living room—ten cannon balls (two of iron and the rest of wood), a broken flintlock musket, Indian tools and a cribbage board found in the blockhouse. He cared for the fort in his own fashion, mending it with shakes and whitewashing the walls, but most of the other structures gradually fell into ruins."

Following Mrs. Davis's death in 1959, the land was acquired by the State of Washington and subsequently deeded to the National Park Service in 1966—though the elderly Crook siblings retained one hundred and seventy acres, including the old house. Jim and his sister Rhoda lived by the parade ground until 1967, when Jim passed away at the age of ninety-three. Afterward, Rhoda lived in the house alone.

Strange tales, naturally, began to swirl about the place. Stories were whispered of a small fortune in gold and banknotes hidden by William Crook shortly before his death; as it turned out, it wasn't a tall tale at all. In 1970, park workers were renovating a barracks building when they discovered an old enamel pot cleverly stashed behind an attic trapdoor. Inside was one thousand, three-hundred and ninety-five dollars in gold coins and paper currency. The cache was presented to ninety-one-year-old Rhoda, who passed away two years later.

Odd tales, too, were told of Masonic rituals performed on the old parade ground—yarns made sinister by talk of strange revelries at the nearby

Afterglow mausoleum. Around four hundred Masons and members of the Eastern Star had indeed gathered at English Camp in the summer of 1919, to consecrate a ritualistic "burying of the hatchet" between the lodges of Friday Harbor, Victoria, and Bellingham. A crimson hatchet was adorned in the American and British colors and ceremonially interred beneath an upraised staff, "bearing on its apex a white dove"— the dove, in Masonic belief, symbolizing sacrifice and rebirth; a burnt offering to the shadowy Light Bearer, according to some.

The Pig War was not the end of swine-related intrigue at English Camp. In October of 1955, a pair of hunters patrolling the surrounding woods spotted a set of knee-bones sticking out from beneath a fallen log. Upon clearing away the leaves and underbrush, a complete human skeleton was found sprawled beside the rusted action of a .22-caliber rifle. All that remained were a few coins, a number of loose bullets, a pair of rubber shoe heels, and a complete set of false teeth. The man had been shot in the right temple with a .22; presumably the same rifle.

Though the scene seemed particularly puzzling, investigators believed it to be the key to solving a fifteen-year-old-mystery. Sheriff Eric Erickson recalled that, in 1940, a man named Lawrence McKay had gone missing from his cabin just a half-mile away. Two years before, McKay had been arrested for stealing and butchering a neighbor's prized brood sow. Sentenced to fifteen years in the state penitentiary, he had been paroled after only two for ill-health.

When McKay had failed to report to the sheriff's office, as he was required to do, deputies were dispatched to his isolated cabin. They found a borrowed automobile parked outside with a hose snaking from the exhaust pipe to an open window—it was deduced that McKay had attempted to kill himself, but the body was nowhere to be found. Erickson now believed that McKay had gone into the woods to finish the job. The irony of a pig-thief's remains being found at a Pig War site was not lost on locals.

The camp's long history of unusual events has led to a variety of ghostly tales. One such yarn was spun by Saltspring Island resident Keith Milliken, who often participated in historical reenactments at English Camp.

"I went to the Encampment every summer since about 1998," said Keith. "I was pretty heavily into reenacting at the time. I was recreating a Royal Marine private named Nehemiah Miles, who was a real character who'd served at English Camp for eight years. He was a shoemaker who'd served in Sebastopol and Canton and a lot of places like that before ending up on San Juan. For the Encampment, we'd set up in rows of canvas bell tents like they would have done in real life, and stay out there for a couple of days doing black powder demonstrations, marching, things like that. A pipe band used to come out and play 'Men of Harlech' and 'A Life on the Ocean Wave.' It was a wonderful time, really.

"It would have been about 2002 or 3, and it was our first night out there. I woke up in the middle of the night, sometime past midnight, and I went out to the portables to take a leak. I just remember how eerie it was—I was in my under-shirt and uniform trousers, dressed like a Marine from the 1860s, and here I was walking across the parade deck of this old place that hadn't hardly changed since Nehemiah Miles was there. It felt like stepping back in time, and I mean *really* back in time. In the dark there wasn't a trace of anything modern.

"Well, crossing the parade deck, I saw there was someone walking towards me, from towards the guardhouse [blockhouse]. I saw he was in uniform, so my first thought was to yell out, 'who goes there,' but then I remembered I wasn't in character! So as he got closer I waved, figuring he could see me in the moonlight. But he didn't wave back, he just kept along. And finally he walked right up to me, and I could get a look at him. He was wearing a Light Infantry uniform the same as mine; full tunic, forage cap, and a Snider-Enfield. I remember it like it was yesterday, because I think I said to myself, 'wow, this guy's kit is a heck of a lot nicer than mine!' I didn't stop to think why this guy would be out wandering around in full get-up.

"He said, 'lend us a fag?', meaning a cigarette, of course. I just happened to smoke at the time, so I gave him one. He didn't ask for a light or anything, he just nodded, gave kind of a grunt of thanks, and

**49**

walked off again, headed out into the woods there. I didn't think all that much of it, just that I hadn't recognized the guy, and it was a little odd that he'd been talking in an English accent, too . . .

"The next day, I asked around looking for the guy, because I wanted to ask him who'd made his uniform—it'd looked a lot nicer than mine and most of the other reenactors'. But all I kept hearing was, 'no, I didn't go out last night,' and 'if I had, I wouldn't have gotten dressed up for it.' Then, sometime that evening, a few friends and I hiked up to the old cemetery on the hill to pay our respects like we usually did. When we got up there, sitting on top of one of the headstones, I found a Du Maurier cigarette—unsmoked, and just like the one I'd given out the night before. The headstone was for a private named James Wensley, who'd drowned in the bay in 1869, as I recall. The marker said they'd never found his body.

"I never did figure out who it was I ran into that night—and I couldn't remember his face, no matter how hard I tried. Maybe I was too focused on his uniform to notice. But, looking back, I can't help but remember how *pale* he was—pale enough that he was practically glowing in the moonlight."

Keith Milliken was not the only visitor to experience strange phenomena at the park. Seasonal park ranger Chris Floyd* had a number of strange tales to report:

"I've actually heard another version of the cigarette story from someone else," said Floyd. "One of the other rangers used to say that, maybe twenty years ago, a tourist had come up to him and said that a guy in full British military uniform had just come out of nowhere and asked for a smoke. The tourist wanted to know if there was a reenactment going on, and of course there wasn't.

"Personally, I've only had one 'ghost' encounter. I was in the blockhouse doing a little maintenance, and I felt something scratch the top of my head—like you might scratch behind a dog's ear. I think I probably screamed like a little girl and got the heck out of there! I still couldn't tell you what that was about. I also heard a bugle call once, on an early morning when it was foggy out, but I wouldn't say that was a ghost, necessarily. Could have been someone really playing a bugle, although I don't know who it would have been."

A visitor named Jamie Henneberger reported phenomena of a similarly-supernatural bent while touring the blockhouse in 2019. The ancient blockhouse had been constructed in 1860, ostensibly as a defensive position against the semi-anticipated American assault. The rifle ports were never used in anger, however, and the strangely-skewed structure instead found use as a stockade. Guards slept on the ground floor, while prisoners were housed in the narrow cells above—usually drunkards or deserters, but on occasion an unruly civilian or two.

"My first and only visit to English Camp was a scary one," reported Hennebeger, who visited with her family. "I experienced a very heavy feeling in my chest when I was inside the [blockhouse]. The air seemed very thick. On the second floor, where the cells were, I had a very quick mental image of a man in a British redcoat standing in the corner. I completely believe there are some spirits left behind in the cells, maybe trapped there. All of the photos I took in there have orbs like I've never seen anywhere else. In one of them, you can see an orb almost perfectly centered over my sister's face. My sister's kid accidentally erased the SD card, though, so I don't have it to show."

Elsewhere, the sounds of drums have been reported, both at night and in the early morning—though not the drums of the British parade ground.

"Some people say they hear Native American drums," says Chris Floyd. "I never did, but we'd get people asking if there was a drum circle nearby or something. There's so much history on that land that we don't even know. It goes back thousands and thousands of years. People had seen lights out on Guss Island once, too, like torches, and heard chanting and drums. No one's supposed to be out there at all, period, because it's sacred to the Lummi tribe [...] and there weren't any Lummi folks visiting that night, either, as far as anyone knew [...] all I can say is, there's a lot of bones buried out there."

Do ghosts wander the terraced hills and formal gardens of English Camp? Does some sort of spiritual power still flow from the otherworldly opening on

Guss Island from which the First Man emerged? One might answer these questions, and others, with a simple walk among the old structures and the weird stones that dot the woods along Garrison Bay.

# Operation Sea Wall

The sinister Circle Trigon Party was a totalitarian regime born out of the ashes of post-war Europe. In June of 1961, their elite shock-troops swarmed down from the north and seized a peninsula belonging to the Republic of Olympia, a democratic nation comprising portions of Whatcom, Skagit, and San Juan Counties. These Trigonist forces dug in and had soon fortified themselves, Normandy-like, along the steep southwestern shore of San Juan Island. Meanwhile, the panicked Olympian government had appealed to the United Nations for help, and the U.S. 4th Infantry Division was called up to intervene.

That was the scenario, anyway, that was dreamed up for "Operation Sea Wall"—a massive combined-arms field exercise that began on Sept-ember 15th, 1961. A week before, the "Aggressor" forces, in actuality an element of the division's 47th Infantry

Regiment, had landed near American Camp and occupied the island from Cattle Point to Cady Mountain.
Now, it was up to the "Liberators" to rout them. The
8th and 39th Infantry Regiments mobilized at Fort
Lewis and piled aboard a fourteen-ship naval convoy
bound for the San Juans.

Among the Aggressors was then-Specialist Bob
Stone*. His company had dug in on the windswept
meadows below Mount Finlayson, overlooking South
Beach and the wild Strait of Juan de Fuca.

"I was in the Recon Platoon," recalled Stone. "We
were a pretty relaxed outfit, which I always liked. I'd
never gone in for the whole spit-polished boot deal.
Some of the Joes liked that sort of thing, but not me.
I joined the Army to do John Wayne stuff, not sit on
my footlocker and shine belt buckles. [...] In Recon,
we usually wore the old World War II field jackets
with the new trousers, and we'd get the mangiest-
looking sandbags we could for our helmet covers.
None of our guns were newer than World War II, I'd
say. I never even touched the M14. We were a real
wild-and-woolly outfit, but that was just the way we
liked it.

"We landed on San Juan about a week before and
set up. It was a nice time—if you were an officer,
anyway. They set up the command post at some
resort cabins a few miles away and took the cabins for
themselves. Us dogfaces set up in tents and foxholes
in the open air. But just about any place beats Yakima,
so we weren't bellyaching too much. Anyway, they

had a field PX and a movie projector, and the PX sold beer.

"The engineers graded a lot of roads and took down fences, things like that. They cleared off the driftwood on the beach there for the tracks and set up smokepots. We dug foxholes all along the coast and some of the guys even made up a sign that said 'Yankees Go Home.' Aggressor duty was always a lot of fun, because we just had to sit there, you know, smoke 'em if you got 'em, and let the poor dumb b—ds come to us."

Indeed, the Army had commandeered thousands of acres of land on San Juan for the exercise, much of it agricultural, and had graded roads and removed fencing to accommodate their armored personnel carriers—the islanders, fortunately, were reported to have been "unusually cooperative." The center of Aggressor operations was the old Mar Vista Resort near False Bay, and their defensive line extended south along the storied beachhead where the landing was to take place.

"You could feel the history all around you," continued Stone. "I'd never even heard of the San Juans, before Sea Wall, but our C.O. told us about the Pig War and all that. Long-winded fella that he was. You could see bits and pieces all over the place just sitting on the ground. I was poking around a cove by the command post and found an old, old shack made out of cedar shakes that had all turned silver in the weather. There was all kinds of stuff inside, old bits of tack and whatnot, but the thing I remember most was a real rusty old branding iron that said 'H.B.C.,' for Hudson's Bay Company. That ought to tell you how old the place was.

"Anyway, we dug into the history, and I mean that literally, when we started digging foxholes. We were spread out along the beachhead for a long ways, and me and my squad were set in close together, below the mountain there towards [Cattle Point]. It's a beautiful coast, kind of like Big Sur. Just big hillsides of grass that looked more like Yakima, almost, but a hell of a lot prettier. Anyways, we started digging holes, and right away we started pulling out all kinds of junk. A guy named Redmond*, in the hole next to mine, found a couple of brass buttons off an old army uniform. They were so old, we figured they must have been from the Pig War days. And we all started digging up charcoal and shards of bone—we couldn't tell what they were from. A few feet down, we hit a layer of seashells.

"Now, we had an Indian guy in our squad named Baldonado*, but we mostly called him 'Chief.' I guess that wouldn't fly these days, but back then it was all good-natured. Chief was half-Indian and half-Mexican [...] I couldn't tell you what tribe, but he'd grown up way out in the boonies on the east side [of the Cascades]. He was a real [...] what you'd call an Indian's Indian, I guess. He'd disappear on weekends, going out into the back forty there on Fort Lewis, and every Sunday he'd come back with a big old blacktail and he'd dress it right there in the barracks [...] Chief was about born for Recon, and we all just respected the hell out of him. So you can imagine what we were thinking when we saw him starting to get kind of spooked.

"I remember he bent down and started sifting through all that junk we were digging out of the holes, and he just said 'there was a village here.' But that was all he'd say. Later on, I heard somebody dug up a skeleton in an army coat. I couldn't tell you how true that is [...] but if a Joe did find something like that, chances are he wouldn't tell anybody. It'd be too much of a snafu with the officers getting involved [...] it'd be less headache just to dig a new hole."

In the days leading up to the attack, the men of Recon Platoon set about creating a Listening Post-Observation Post farther down the slopes toward South Beach. They excavated a hole large enough for two or three men and heaped up sandbags and brush and strung up a length of camouflage netting. At the post was a medium machine gun—to be fired "notionally," of course —and a field radio. Their assignment was to scan the seas and report any signs of Liberator activity.

"There was no night vision in those days," said Stone. "So, what that meant for us was a lot of long nights staring off into the dark and really *listening*. We'd been told—or, I should say, we'd heard it through the E-4 grapevine—that there were going to be Navy frogmen coming ashore before dawn, the morning of the attack. So, the night we went tactical, all of us were on high alert. Specialist So-And-So told PFC Whos-It that these frogmen liked to beat up the Joes they captured—no play acting for the UDT [Underwater Demolition Team] boys, apparently. So we had clubs and bayonets ready to go. I remember I said to my buddy Brandt*, I said 'I'm not about to get disarmed and smacked around by some g—d d—d squid. If some frogman tries to creep up on me I'll unload that A6 [machine gun, loaded with blanks] right in his face and blind the son of a b—h.' Of course, what happened ended up being a lot more bizarre.

"They tried to keep the whole thing as realistic as they could by not telling us exactly when the attack was going to happen. That first night, around two in the morning, me and Brandt left the bivouac and went down to the listening post to pull guard. We had a hell of a time just getting down there, I remember. Like I said, we'd gone tactical, so we couldn't use flashlights or anything like that. Just the moonlight, and the moon was full. Made that whole grassy meadow running along the coast there kind of glow. Finally we got down there, and right away it seemed kind of *off*.

"It was Jack Royce* and a kid named Tuttle* who'd been pulling guard for the past couple hours before us. The post was kind of scooped into the hillside, so me and Brandt slid down into the hole on our asses and the kid Tuttle about jumped out of his skin. Royce just looked at me real deadpan-like and said 'you scared the s—t out of Tuttle.' I said to him, kind of half-joking, 'what the h—l are you two jokers so worked up about, anyway? Frogmen giving you trouble?' He said no, but they'd been hearing things moving around in the grass, like footsteps. I said to him, 'well, did you see any-one?' and he said no. They'd been on edge because they figured it was either frogmen creeping up from the beach or it was an officer coming to jack with them, to see if they were asleep. I figured they were just tired and hearing things, and maybe it was a deer or something at most. I said to Royce, 'hey, listen here, buddy, we're soldiers of the Circle Trigon, and we're not afraid of no [expletive] frogmen *or* butter-bars.' He just mumbled something like 'yeah, yeah, good luck' and him and the kid headed out.

"That was a hell of a view at that post, even at night. It was a harvest moon, big and gold, I remember, and it looked like it was about a mile away [...] close enough to see it was made out of cheddar, anyway. From that point there you could see about twenty miles across the strait to the Peninsula and all the city lights from Port Townsend and Angeles and all the towns out that way. And right there to the east, a lot closer, was Victoria, Canada. So with all the city lights and the moon and everything, there was about as good of [illumination] as you could ask for.

"I wrapped myself up good and warm in my poncho and lay down prone, looking out through a gap in the sandbags next to Brandt—he was on the gun and I had the radio. Finally, I said 'get some sleep, I'll keep an eye on things.' I'd take the first hour and he could take the second. So he racked out and I hopped on the A6. I felt pretty awake, I remember, and I made sure to pack a lip so I didn't pass out later.

"Maybe thirty minutes into my watch I started hearing s—t [...] it was the same as Royce said. I could've sworn I heard someone crunching through the dry grass, just one slow step at a time. Couldn't tell if it was behind us, or below, or what, just that there was someone out there. I kicked Brandt and whispered to him that we had company, and he woke up with kind of a start, like I'd scared him. He seemed pretty out of it, but he pulled up his M1 and got out his club in case it was the frogmen. We were ready for 'em if it was.

"We had a challenge and pass, like you see in the D-Day movies—you know, 'flash-thunder.' I forget what ours was that night, but I called out the challenge word and didn't get a response. I said it one more time and got nothing, so I looked at Brandt and said 'okay, we're in business.' But, on the off-chance it was a deer, I sure as hell didn't want to be the jackass firing off a belt and waking up the whole company over nothing. And something stopped me from

**61**

calling higher [command]—so we just set still and listened.

"It was the d—ndest thing I ever heard. It sounded like something on two legs walking up on us, kind of stealthily, and it always sounded like it was getting closer—but it never did. I don't know how else to explain it. Then Brandt grabbed my arm and said, 'who the hell is that?'

"He was looking behind us, back up the hill to our right. I turned my head and saw what he was looking at right away. There was a guy standing there in the moonlight, maybe thirty yards out, give or take. We didn't say nothing, we just looked at him—and the more we looked, the less it made sense. He was a bigger guy, over six feet, and he was wearing a big-brimmed hat and some kind of overcoat. And being in the moonlight, we could see other little details too, like that he was wearing some kind of shoulder belt with a shiny buckle, like you'd see on a Civil War soldier, or a Pig War soldier.

"Now, you might be expecting me to say that he was see-through, or something like that, but he wasn't—he looked pretty solid to me, and I figured either a Cav Scout got hopelessly lost [...] or this was some kind of farmer or something, lost or come to screw with us. So I called up higher [command] and said, you know, 'one actual, we got a bogie at our five o'clock.' I described what we were seeing, and our lieutenant sent down a little patrol to see what we were smoking on. By the time they got to the listening post, maybe half an hour later, we were all pretty spooked. We watched them come down from the hill and pretty much just walk right past the mystery guy—I mean they *had* to have seen him. He was standing still the whole time, and they came within ten feet of him. 'Course, we didn't have comms with the patrol, so we couldn't tell them that. Our platoon sergeant was leading it, and I think he was kind of p—sed at having to roll out of the sack, but by the time he got down to us he looked a little pale himself. Said they hadn't seen anything, of course, but they'd run into a wall of cold air that was cold enough that they could see their breath. Keep in mind, it was [...] mid-September, and there was a chilly breeze coming off the water—but nothing to freeze a guy's breath. Anyway, when the guys all got to the listening post, I took my eyes off the mystery man for a second, just a split second, and when I looked back he was gone [...] we chalked it up to a civvie [civilian] who got into the training area [...] there's your ghost story, huh?"

The rest of the night was comparatively uneventful for Specialists Stone and Brandt. The pair were relieved early by two members of the patrol, and the group returned to the bivouac area to catch a few hours of sleep before the scheduled attack. When the UDT frogmen *did* come, it was to "notionally" clear the beach of driftwood, using explosives, for the landing craft and amphibious vehicles—in reality, the Aggressor forces had done the work days earlier, and the "explosives" were simply smokepots, which also doubled as a smokescreen for the attack. At 7:30 a.m., on the 15th, a squadron of Air Force F-100 Su-per Sabres "strafed" the Trigonist defenses as the first waves of landing craft and amphibious assault vehicles put ashore on South Beach with the rising tide. The frogmen stood by and acted as lifeguards. Meanwhile, groups of San Juan Islanders and schoolchildren—who'd gotten the morning off—gathered on the bleachers set up along Mount Finlayson to watch the events unfold. Five thousand men had landed on South Beach.

Stone's platoon and the rest of the Trigonists battled it out on the sunny slopes. Machine guns ripped and rifle-fire, made hollow-sounding by the blank cartridges, popped and crackled like fire-works to the delighted onlookers. M47 Pattons roared over the anti-tank pits and exchanged fire with Aggressor armor. By 8:30, the defenders had been driven from their foxholes and were retreat-ing north towards the command post at False Bay. "It was a hell of a slog, with all my gear and me humping an A-bag [equip-ment] for the A6, too," recalled Stone. "Some guys got made casualties right away and sat the whole thing out. I wasn't so lucky."

The Trigonists were pushed north nearly ten miles to Cady Mountain, a rough and forested region more similar to the ranges at Fort Lewis. The men defended this final redoubt for two full days, and even managed to launch a nuclear strike—simulated with smokepots and burning gasoline—before a surrender was signed at two p.m. that Monday. Operation Sea Wall had come to a close, and the next few days would be spent "police-calling" the battleground for spent shell casings.

"We had a lot of time to B.S., walking shoulder-to-shoulder looking for brass," said Stone. "We got to talking about the days before the attack. For one thing, Brandt told me that he'd been so shook up when I woke him that night because he'd been having the worst nightmare of his life. He was dreaming that a black shadow was standing over him, about to pull him off into the dark, but he couldn't move or yell or anything. So when he saw that spooky-looking guy staring at us, he'd been scared [out of his mind], because it was like the nightmare coming to life.

"Turns out, a lot of the guys had been having dreams like that—the kind where you're frozen and there's something evil creeping around. Guys were saying they'd never had dreams like that before, and they never did after we left, either. Another guy said he'd felt something yank on his pack during one of our night movements through the woods, but he'd been in the rear, and there wasn't anyone behind him. Who knows [...] lot of history on that island."

Bob Stone went on to serve seven more years in the Army, including a tour in Vietnam with the 196th Light Infantry Brigade—where, he says, he encountered man-eating snakes in the remote jungle rivers. But that, as he admits, is "a whole other story."

As for the supposed spooks above South Beach, who can say . . . with so much history saturated into the land itself, from Indian villages at Cattle Point to murder and mayhem around American Camp, the idea of a haunting or two is hardly unimaginable. Stone's story of an unearthed skeleton is even seemingly corroborated by a strange discovery just a few months later. A trio of rabbit hunters—Terry and Ready Kuchenreuter, and Bill Farnsworth—discovered a human skeleton buried near American Camp, on land that had been occupied by Sea Wall troops. Investigators also discovered brass buttons from a U.S. Army uniform and a few deteriorated bits of a blue coat, leading some to brand the remains as being that of a Pig War soldier. Were the bones found in a filled-in foxhole? The exact location of the find, unfortunately, has been long forgotten.

# UFOs and Other Phenomena

The existence of UFOs in the San Juans is undeniable. An *unidentified* flying object could be anything from a satellite to a stray balloon; though many of the strange sightings that have surfaced in recent years seem to indicate a phenomenon that is anything but mundane, or even explainable in terms of known science.

Take, for example, Jim Dunn's inexplicable encounter on a dark winter evening in 2015. According to the *Journal of the San Juans*, Dunn and his wife were headed to a lecture at the Friday Harbor Laboratories at around 6:15 when they spotted a trio of orange orbs in the sky over Mullis Street. At first, Dunn had assumed the lights to be that of a small aircraft making a "very low approach" to the nearby airport—but there was "something weird about the movements," and Dunn decided to pull over and take a closer look.

"It was three orange lights moving independently," said Dunn. "At first I rationalized it was a drone, but they were moving too rapidly for a drone."

Dunn was understandably unnerved, and soon contacted the Air Traffic Control Division at Naval Air Station Whidbey Island to find out if anything out of the ordinary had been reported. According to Dunn, there *had* been a helicopter in the area, but forty-five minutes *after* the sighting. The day after that, Dunn filed an official report with the National UFO Reporting Center (NUFORC), which read:

*I stopped our car so we could watch since the lights were starting to bob up and down. I said they had to be helicopters. But then they almost appeared to be going down behind the buildings in town. They stopped getting closer and suddenly started climbing at a very high speed headed back northwest. They grew dimmer and one at a time, blinked out and were gone. The whole duration of this sighting was about two minutes. I kept trying to find an explanation for what we were seeing. I wish I had immediately reached for my iPhone to get a video. I knew they were unconventional aircraft since they didn't have red and green navigation lights. Then the erratic flight and changing speed ruled out any aircraft I have ever seen. My wife and I are both private pilots and have flown into the Friday Harbor airport hundreds of times.*

"It's got to be from another world," said Dunn. "It's nothing I could rationalize."

Dunn's sighting, as it turned out, was only the most publicized—San Juan Islanders had been reporting bizarre aerial phenomena for decades, and the pattern had simply gone unnoticed. Eighty-one years before, the *Friday Harbor Journal* had carried an odd little piece reading: "Mr. and Mrs. George Hastin, of Lopez Island, saw a meteor of some kind traveling at a great rate of speed toward the northwest. It was of an odd shape, being straight across the top and rounding at the bottom. It was the color of the sun, covered by smoke."

Forty-three years later, in July of 1977, five islanders reportedly sighted a UFO over Jackson Beach, just south of Friday Harbor. Norval Cunningham described an "object of light" that gave "an impression of brightness, of red and white." According to Cunningham, the object "moved from horizon to horizon at an elevation estimated at 2,000 feet and an arc of 20 degrees in only 4 or 5 seconds." Though he conjectured that it was a "vehicle" of some type, he was adamant that the object was no earthly aircraft.

Around eight years after that, a pair of off-duty Airmen encountered a mind-bending display near Friday Harbor that defied logical explanation:

"In 1984 or 85 I was rabbit hunting on [San Juan Island] with an Air Force buddy. We were tent camping somewhere on the island. I don't remember the date or even the time of year; probably late summer or fall.

"After dark I was in the tent and he called me outside to see something strange. I noticed that a fairly bright light was illuminating him and he was looking in the direction of the light. I turned and saw what looked like an illuminated globe fairly high in the sky. Its angular diameter was slightly larger than a full moon. It was somewhat brighter than a full moon. It was featureless, just a globe of light. There was no way to judge the distance, or actual size.

"As we watched, it was slowly descending. There was no sound associated with it. In the time I viewed it, it descended from an angular position higher than forty-five degrees to a low of about thirty degrees. At that time an identical globe appeared to its left, gradually brightening over several seconds to the same brightness as the first one, which a short time later gradually dimmed and was no longer visible. Then the second globe began ascending, again with no audible sound. When it reached an angular altitude of perhaps sixty degrees it dimmed and was no longer visible. With both globes the only motion we perceived was vertical. We were dumbfounded and have never heard any sort of explanation, although we guessed it to be some sort of military object."

Around twelve years later, a similarly dramatic "close encounter" was reported by a local high school science teacher:

"I was sitting in my front room by a south-facing

window a little before 9:30. I was alone as it was a Wednesday and my wife was with her quilting group. A bright greenish object streaked into view moving south and was visible for a few seconds until it disappeared over the horizon to the south. The object had the appearance of re-entering space debris from my location. The speed was constant and the direction of travel never changed from my vantage point. I assumed it was a rocket booster or satellite burning up in the atmosphere, as it resembled a re-entering Russian booster I had witnessed some years previous. I mentioned the object to my wife, and the next day heard reports that it was space junk and dismissed the sighting as such."

Nevertheless, the teacher filed the sighting with NUFORC at the behest of the organization's director, who had heard the story personally and deemed it worthy of recording. Many less scientifically-structured reports were also made in the years leading up to the Jim Dunn incident—one 2005 report concerned a UFO that "swooped down from the sky, dropped an object, and then sped back up into the clouds." According to the witness,

"I was standing out in the field outside of my house when I felt a buzzing sensation in my skull. I looked up and there was a strange object that descended from the clouds. It was oval shaped and it had a strange yellow luminescence coming off of it. It seemed to have dropped a glowing white object into a nearby field, and immediately took off. After it was gone, the buzzing ceased. I went to try and find the glowing object in the nearby field and I only found a dent in the ground. The dent was not a hole. The ground and the grass appeared to be perfectly intact, except that it was a concave dent."

Other tales have been told of military aircraft appearing to pursue these UFOs over the San Juans— one islander sighted a group of fighters "pointlessly" chasing a large, silvery disc for several miles, before the object "went straight up and dwindled to the size of a pin just before it vanished in the stratosphere." Such reports may not be as far-fetched as they seem at face-value, however. In 2019, a U.S. Navy spokes-man stated that "There have been incursions into our training ranges. Pilots are seeing things that shouldn't be there because it's restricted air space," adding, "It's all about safety and security."

The San Juan witness went on to note, "[the UFO] was completely noiseless, although many seconds later the sound of the jets reached us. The object traveled very quietly. Wouldn't that make airports nicer to live near?"

Unbeknownst to many, UFO sightings in the San Juans stretch as far back as the First World War— though these tales took on a considerably different tone than the typical "extraterrestrial" explanation. Prior to Roswell and the famed Kenneth Arnold incident of 1947, UFOs had usually been called "ghost rockets" or "foo fighters." Allied airmen had reported them in the skies over Europe as balls of green or orange light that tailed their aircraft on night missions and never appeared on radar; many believed the lights to have been a highly secretive German "wonder weapon," though records of such a weapon, or its purpose, were never found. When the phenomena failed to cease after the war, however, a new belief emerged that the lights were advanced spy-planes piloted by the Soviets and designed by captured German scientists—or flown by the Arctic-based Germans themselves, according to some.

The character of these "UFOs," in other words, seemed to be dictated by the general paranoia of the times. And during World War I, in the British Dominion of Canada, the widespread paranoia was of a potential invasion by the German Empire. Mysterious, unidentified "aero-planes and airships" were widely reported across the nation during the early years of the war, as evidenced by numerous newspaper accounts and intelligence reports. There was considerable fear amongst the Canadian populace of spies and infiltrators slipping across the wide border with the then-neutral United States; just days after the declaration of war in August of 1914, the city of Niagara Falls was seized by rumors of a looming air-raid, as local militiamen had reported the "whirring of an aeroplane" in the pre-dawn hours. Soon after, a panic swept Ottawa when pedes-trians near Parliament Hill "thought they saw an airship with a bright light." The light was determined to be a bright star or planet. By 1915, the fears had further increased into a fever-pitch; that February, headlines in Ottawa screamed: "Ottawa In Darkness Awaits Aeroplane Raids", "Several Aeroplanes Make a Raid into the Dom-inion of Canada", "Entire City of Ottawa in Darkness, Fearing Bomb-Droppers", "Machines Crossed St. Lawrence River, Passing Over Brookville—Two Over Gananoque—Seen by Many Citizens, Heading for the Capital—One Was Equipped with Powerful Searchlights—Fire Balls Dropped." The Mayor himself claimed to have "been caught in the glare of the aeroplane's most powerful searchlight." The next morning, the remains of two paper hot-air balloons were recovered, equipped with flares and firecrackers—the work of American pranksters.

In wartime British Columbia, aircraft of any kind were a virtual unknown; perhaps explaining why F. Ashley Sparkes, headmaster of the Victoria Preparatory School, came running when one of his students called out "Look at the aeroplane!" on the morning of January 16th, 1917. Sparkes observed a single biplane circling over nearby Oak Bay for a total of five minutes, before the plane headed south and across the U.S. border. After a brief investigation, the Superintendent of the Provincial Police wired Sir Percy Sherwood, Chief Commissioner of Dominion Police, stating:

"On instruction from Attorney General, I beg to report that a biplane was seen circling over Oak Bay, Victoria, at noon on sixteenth instant. Came from direction of San Juan Island and disappeared going south. No aircraft in British Columbia connected with this flight; there are at least five machines in Seattle, Wash., capable of making this flight."

The shaken Canadians made a formal complaint to the American government soon after, protesting further aerial incursions.

Another, even stranger encounter would surface in Victoria just a week later. A woman reportedly sighted a pair of aircraft in the wee hours of the morning, and, more surprisingly, "heard the pilots talking to each other in a foreign language." The report was passed on to the Dominion Police, though an intelligence officer noted that it was "so absurd and impossible that no credence can be placed in it." It was an incident that the Americans couldn't be blamed for, either.

# Cry Baby House

Vague legends once swirled around a vacant farmhouse on False Bay Road—an ancient and weatherbeaten house, turned grey in the salt air, that had stood at the end of a long and flower-flanked driveway since the early 1880s. No one was exactly sure of the home's history, even the longtime islanders who could recall the night it burned, on Halloween, 1974. Most could agree that a Mrs. Smith had lived there in the 1940s, a kindly woman who never let a child pass by without offering milk and cookies—regardless of whether the child was alive or not.

"I remember people saying that Mrs. Smith used to leave out milk and cookies for a little ghost girl that would appear every night. Some people said it was

Mrs. Smith's little sister, who'd died in the house as a kid, or it was her daughter, who'd died there, too," said lifelong islander Craig Wilton*. "I don't think anyone really knew."

In truth, the cedar-framed house had been constructed by Peter and Kristina Smith, immigrants from Germany who had settled on San Juan in the 1870s. Kristina had come over first, to decide whether the island would be to her liking. It was, and the couple had lived there for many decades; the last of which Mrs. Smith spent caring for her invalided husband.

Following Mrs. Smith's death, a succession of renters and full-time residents lived at the house — many of whom reported spine-tingling phenomenon, such as the spectral sound of a phantom infant crying in the night.

"We always called it the Cry Baby House," said Craig. "A guy who lived there in the fifties moved out after just a few weeks because he'd hear a baby crying somewhere upstairs when the place was empty."

Other tales were told, too, of a phantom woman seen wandering False Bay Road searching for her lost child, and of a ghostly black car that terrorized motorists passing near the home on certain dark nights.

"My brother and his friends ran into the car," according to Craig. "They were out cruising one night, oh, fifty, fifty-five years ago, and a black sedan started following them. It got up right behind them with its high-beams on and was being real aggressive. So my brother sped up, to get the car to back off, and took his eyes off the rearview mirror for just a second. He looked back, and the car was gone. That stretch of road was a straightaway, and there wasn't anywhere that car could have turned off so quickly. Just a ditch and farm fields on both sides."

Other tales often told of the Cry Baby House included buried gold in the field, ghostly orbs of light, objects moving of their own accord, and the apparition of a woman appearing on the staircase. Teenage thrill-seekers, drawn by these tantalizing tidbits, would frequently congregate at the abandoned house in the early 1970s—the most popular time being Halloween Night, when teens would light candles and break out Ouija boards for devil's hour terror-sessions.

One participant in these late-night escapades was then-sixteen-year-old Terri Vollmer*, who claims to have been present at the Cry Baby House's fiery destruction on Halloween Night, 1974.

"It was a school night, so I wasn't thrilled about staying out late," recalled Terri. "But my sister [Lori] dragged me along, her and a couple of her friends and a couple of boys. She had a Ouija board that she'd been wanting to try out—it was a creepy looking thing, and us being Catholic, we weren't even supposed to have one. My mother would have thrown a fit if she'd known. But Lori had gotten it at King's with her babysitting money and she wanted to try it out in a place where, I guess, she'd be the most likely to talk to something. And on San Juan, at the time, there was really only one obvious spot to do that—which was the Cry Baby House.

"It was an old, old farmhouse that must have been over a hundred years old. The paint was mostly gone by then, and a lot of the windows were broken [...] there was a big dried-out wasp nest in the kitchen, I remember. The place had been empty for a few years and it was for sale at the time. I don't know who would have bought it, but it was for sale. I think rabbit hunters used to use it for a shelter.

"A friend of Lori's brought a bunch of candles and we set them up in the old living room. I don't know what time it was, but it was dark, and the only light was from the candles and a flashlight or two.

"Someone had burned a pentagram into the floor, with a blowtorch or something, maybe. We avoided that, because none of us were into devil-worship or anything like that. We sat on the floor around the board and the five of them put their fingers on the [planchette] except for me. I just sat back and watched because I was already scared enough as it was. Then the first thing they said was, 'is there a spirit here who'd like to speak to us?' and the thing went to 'YES.'

"Lori asked what it's name was, and it spelled out 'MAMA.' I think someone asked if it was Mama Cass Elliot, from the Mamas and the Papas, who had just died a few months before, and it shot to 'NO' right away. Very fast, almost like it was offended. It spelled out 'MAMA MAMA MAMA' over and over again.

Finally, someone asked it if 'Mama' had died in the house—I guess we were still assuming it was human. It said 'NO.' Then someone asked, I think, if 'Mama' wanted to tell us anything. They probably didn't know what else to ask. It said 'LOOKING FOR LOST GIRL.' I don't know about everyone else, but my first thought was the stories you'd hear about the Cry Baby House, and the woman people would see who was looking for her lost child—or the old lady who'd leave out milk and cookies for the ghost girl. So, someone asked 'what girl?' and it replied very quick. It said, 'ANY OF YOU.'

"Now, at this point, I don't think there was anything I wanted more in the world than to leave that house—but I was probably too afraid to leave the candlelight, anyway. Everyone started arguing, accusing each other of moving the [planchette]. Finally, one of the boys—Bobby Kennard*, I think—said, 'Okay Mama, if you're real, then give us a sign. Make the flames flare up,' talking about the candles. Well, nothing happened. But I think we'd all had enough Ouija for one night, so they said 'Goodbye' on the board and we packed up and blew out the candles and left.

"I'll never forget it. We were half-way down the driveway in Lori's V.W. when someone said, 'oh my god, look!' She stopped the car and we all craned our necks around. There was a glow, an orange glow, that was starting to fill all the windows of the house—and then we saw the flames. Bobby, I think it was Bobby, said 'punch it, get out of here,' and we did.

"No one was ever arrested for arson or anything like that. None of our names ever came up, and, to tell you the truth, I never had any particular guilt [...] because I knew, deep down, that none of us had really set that fire intentionally, or at all. We hadn't left any candles burning in there, or cigarettes, or anything—and maybe it was a good thing that it had burned. It didn't seem like anyone could live there for very long, anyway."

Though the old Cry Baby House is now just a slight depression in the earth, marked by the dual-rows of daffodils that appear in the springtime to mark the old drive, it needn't be the end of the terrifying old traditions—perhaps the ghost car still tailgates passersby on dark nights, while "Mama" lurks somewhere in the black fields, searching for "LOST GIRLS" or other unfortunate souls . . .

# *Kanaka Joe*

For years after the murders, any and all bloody
incidents in the Puget Sound region were referred to
as "the worst since Kanaka Joe." In 1872, an old man
named William Fuller had gone missing from his
lonely farm on the west side of San Juan—and, in the
summer of the next year, a young couple and their
unborn child were found brutally slain in their new
home. The killings, though hardly the island's first,
were a kind of "loss of innocence" for the fledgling
frontier community; a far-cry from whiskey-fueled
violence of yesteryear, and a tragedy that would echo
down through the years in whispered tales of the
horror near Mount Dallas.

Lila Hannah Firth was eighty years old when she
wrote an account of her childhood on San Juan,

spanning from 1870 to the mid-1880s. She had been seven years old when the first murder occurred.

"My father, James Hannah, and my mother, Minerva, landed on San Juan Island in October of 1864," she wrote. "They came across from Victoria in a large Indian canoe with two sons, my older brothers, who were born in California. One year later I came into the family; 2 ½ years later my brother Henry was born. So there we were, the four of us children to grow up in that wild country, full of Indians. But no wild animals that would harm us, thank the Lord for that. We ran carefree all through the woods and over the hills.

"One thing that frightened me though was, now and then, we would meet a big, kinky-haired, black-faced Kanaka. Seemed to me the woods were quite full of them going and coming, hither and thither, through the little trails in the woods."

The "Kanakas" were Native Hawaiians, who had been brought to the Northwest as laborers by the Hudson's Bay Company in the early 19th century. Many of them had once worked at the company's Belle Vue farm, near Cattle Point, and had stayed on the island after the farm's dissolution, marrying Indian women and settling at the titular Kanaka Bay. Friday Harbor had been named for one of these men, a sheepherder named Joe Friday who had lived on the present-day townsite.

Lila continued,

"Another old Kanaka with his family and a number of his friends moved out to a point near our home, I would guess about one-and-a-half miles from our place, the Hannah Farm. There was a great long point of land that went out into the Strait of Juan de Fuca. After this colony settled in there the settlers named it Kanaka Point. Out near the end of the point on the north side there was quite a sheltered bay where boats could lie at anchor in any kind of bad storms, which are quite severe on the Strait at times. That was named Kanaka Bay.

"Well, this other old Kanaka I started to tell you about was named Nuanna. His wife was an Indian and they had a family. The two older boys we came to know quite well. The eldest was named Joe, the second, Kye. Quite often these two boys would stroll up our way, and as my two older brothers were about their age, they would stop and play around our pond with my brothers.

"One morning [in 1873] this Joe Nuanna came to our house. He wanted to borrow a gun from one of my brothers. He said he was going pigeon hunting. They let him have their shotgun. He asked for some shot, too; he said he already had powder and caps. They gave him their little shot pouch that Mother had made for them to carry in their pockets.

"In those days they had to load their guns with powder and shot and a little paper wadding, and they used a ramrod to load the gun. Cartridges were a rare thing; we seldom saw one.

"So off Joe went. That evening when he came to return the gun he did not come to the house. He stood out around the pond and kept whistling. Mother happened to be out doing some chores and she heard him. She came in and said to me, 'Lila, the boys are not here and Joe is out at the pond whistling. You had better see what he wants.'

"So I went skipping over to the pond. He hurried toward me and handed me the shotgun, whirled around and went off in a hurry. I stood there sort of dumb for a moment. Then I called to him.

"I said, 'Joe what did you kill?'

"He answered, 'oh, nothing. Just a few pigeons.'

"Well, I thought, where are they? He had nothing to show for it. He had empty hands and no game that I could see. So I took the gun to the house and told Mother how strange he acted. She put the gun away in the corner with the other guns and no more was said."

Though Minerva Hannah had apparently not thought much of the incident at the time, its connection to the bloody happenings at the Dwyer place—as well as the murder of William Fuller the year before—would soon become clear.

"Our neighbor southeast of us along the water-front was an old Englishman by the name of Fullar [sic]. He had a full claim there that joined Father's line fence. He was a very proud man; shaved his face in such a peculiar way! He shaved his mustache and the front of his face down as far as the end of his chin. From the ears down the back of his chin he left a full beard. He seemed to keep that part trimmed about two inches long.

"Anyway, he had a full claim that joined Father's line fence southeast along the waterfront. He had a few sheep on it but never did any farming. He appeared in every way to be a man of means.

"When he dressed up and went places he looked very classy. He always wore a stove-pipe hat, the kind men wore in those days. So he was looked upon as a man of means with plenty to live on.

"One day a neighbor or friend called on Mr. Fullar. He was not home, but his doors were all open. His little dog 'Jinnie' acted very much distressed. The visitor searched all over the place and then went back home. He couldn't keep Mr. Fullar off his mind and the conditions around the place. Next day he went again to his place and found everything the same.

"Then he raised an alarm throughout the neighborhood and a bunch of people gathered and decided to send for the sheriff, who at that time was Mr. [Stephen] Boyce Sr. He lived out in San Juan Valley and he came immediately. The search continued for several days.

"Finally, with the help of little Jinnie, his dog, they found Mr. Fullar in a fern flat under a large Madrona tree—murdered! Large heavy rocks had been thrown all over his head and most of his body was covered with those monster rocks. It's a scene I shall never forget. I was right there when he was found. My folks must have taken me along in the search, fearing to leave me home. On investigation they found that Mr. Fullar had been shot through the head and had fallen there and then the murderer had thrown all of those rocks upon him.

"Can you ever imagine what a shock that was to our neighborhood? In fact to the whole Island. No clue could be found though they knew his house had been robbed the way things were upset, as he was always such a neat old bachelor and kept his house in perfect order. The suspicion was that he was killed for his money. A coffin was made for him by one of the neighbors. He was laid to rest on his own place in a pretty little fir grove on the bank, down near his beach.

"I remember his funeral service so well. That big old Kanaka, Joe Nuanna, stood right beside me. He was always hanging around my brothers, and I never liked him. As I said before, no clue was found. A big reward was offered for the murderer of Mr. Fullar, still nothing came of it."

Harry Dwyer was a Nova Scotia man who had previously freighted San Juan produce between Victoria and Kanaka Bay aboard his sloop. It had been a lucrative practice; he was known to frequently carry twenty-dollar gold pieces in his pocket. In 1872, the year of the Fuller killing, Dwyer gave up the shipping business and bought a farm on the western flanks of Mount Dallas. He also married a twenty-year-old Victoria woman named Selena and then subsequently turned out his common- law wife, a Haida woman named Ellen.

"The place that Dwyer bought consisted mostly of swamp land," Lila continued. "All that was under cultivation was this meadow land. On a knoll above this meadow sat his house, barn and outhouses. From his house or front porch one could see all over his field, which was a very pretty setting from the house. Out back of his house was some very heavy timber land, ranging up toward the mountain.

"By the following spring of 1873 Harry had secured a team of horses and was all ready to start farming as soon as his meadows were dry enough to plow. In the meantime, Harry had sold his sloop down at Kanaka Bay to another man.

"One afternoon in mid-May, Mother and I were sitting out on our porch off the dining room when we noticed someone coming across our field at a terrible fast pace.

"Mother rose to her feet and took a good look. She said, 'It's Mr. Terrell [a neighbor] I do believe. Wonder what is the matter. He is running!'

"Sure enough. When he got to us, he was so out of breath that he couldn't talk till he sat down and rested for a few minutes. Then he told us that he had just been over to Harry Dwyer's and found Harry murdered. He was lying in the furrow where he was plowing, face down, with a hole in his head! Mr. Terrell said, 'It looks like he has been there for several days. The team still stands there hitched to the plow.

"Mother said to Mr. Terrell, 'Do you think you will be able to go over and get Sheriff Boyce right away?'

"He said maybe he could ride over the hill on horseback.

"Mother said, 'Well, you do that, and I will go over and see if I can find Mrs. Dwyer.'

"She loaned Mr. Terrell a horse to ride into town for the sheriff. My father was away at the time. It was her grim duty to see if she could help the poor wife.

"So my mother took me and started off to the Dwyer home. In going to their house we had to cross the field in which Harry lay dead. We went toward the team of horses—and there was a terrible scene that I shall never forget:

"The horses had dug out great holes in the ground, but they could not go because the reins were around Harry's shoulders, and they were fastened to the bridle bits. They could not pull that weight with their mouths. Harry was a very large man and he had fallen face down in the furrow. We could see the dry blood all over the back of his neck and the green flies were just swarming around him.

"Mother and I hurried up to the house. The doors were all open and we walked in. There on the floor beside the bed lay Mrs. Dwyer, dead. Her face was all black and blue. There was dried blood on her nose and mouth. Had we not known it must be her, we never would have recognized her.

"Out on the front porch were some baby clothes scattered about where it seemed she had been sewing. They were expecting a baby that summer and no doubt she was sitting there sewing when her husband was shot, as from there she could have seen him plowing in the meadow.

"Mother turned to me and said, 'Come on, let's strike for home. This is the sheriff's work. It's no place for us.' So we went back home heartsick. Those scenes just haunted us day and night. Father was in Olympia as he had previously been elected representative from San Juan County to the Legislature. There was mother all alone with we children and wondering who could have committed such a crime, and who would be the next victims?

"Who-who-who—like the night call of an owl kept ringing in her ears. Who could do such a terrible thing? And why? That was the next question. Mother would go about murmuring her thoughts to me in this way:

" 'You know, Lila, we all know that that old man Fullar was murdered for his money. Now could it be possible, do you think, that the Dwyers were murdered for the same purpose? He seemingly had made his stake and married and retired in a way. He had just sold his boat for a good sum of money and who would know all this?'

"Then the thought of the Kanaka Bay camp came into her mind. The wheels in her thoughts started revolving around and around. She thought the bunch over and Joe Nuanna came uppermost in her mind. Could it be possible?

"She said, 'No. He has known Harry Dwyer since he was a small boy. Could he ever do such a terrible thing as that for money?'

"Still the thought stayed with her. Then came the thought of him borrowing our gun about the stated time of the murder and the very queer way he acted when he brought the gun home that evening. Mother became so excited over these thoughts that she went and picked up the gun and took it to the door in a good light and to examine it. She found there was dried blood on the stock of the gun and she knew well that was not there before Joe borrowed the gun. So putting two and two together, she thought she had evidence enough to send for the sheriff and tell him she thought she had a clue to the Dwyer murder.

"She did that. He came over immediately and Mother told him this whole story of her suspicions and showed him the blood stains on the gun stock and said how queer Joe had acted when he returned the gun.

"Mr. Boyce went right down to the Kanaka camp and visited them all—just a social call. He discovered Joe Nuanna was not there. Indian Jim [or Charley] and Joe had departed for Victoria in their canoe. The date worked out well with the date of the murder. Sheriff Boyce came right back to us and asked Mother for the gun Joe had borrowed. He said he was going to follow those two. With the gun he went to Victoria and turned it over to a chemist to have the blood examined. They found it to be human blood.

"By this time the horrible murder had been noised around Victoria. The Dwyers had been Victoria people originally. The authorities on the British side were up and ready to get that chap as soon as they heard of the suspicions. They were not long in rounding up Nuanna and handing him over to our Sheriff."

The Victoria constables had found Nuanna walking casually down Yates Street—and, upon raiding Indian Charley's shack on Humboldt Str-eet, had found a pocket watch belonging to Harry Dwyer. Meanwhile, Sheriff Boyce had recovered a shot pouch at the scene of the crime; the very same pouch that Nuanna had borrowed from the Hannahs. Nuanna was extradited to the United States, and the pouch would become an important piece of evidence at his Port Townsend trial.

"As soon as the court was ready for his trial, the sheriff sent for my mother. She said perhaps they might want to ask me some questions, but they didn't need me. They had plenty of proof to convict him," wrote Lila.

"At the trial in the courtroom, Mother was asked if there was a little bag of shot that went with the gun.

"Mother said, 'Well, I had made a little shot pouch for the boys to carry in their pockets and they might have let Joe have it that day he borrowed the gun.'

"The lawyer said, 'You say you made this bag. What kind of material did you make it of?'

"Mother said, 'Buckskin.'

" 'Will you tell the court just how it was made?' Mother said, 'Yes. First my son found a cartridge shell and he would put a cork in the other end of the shell and that would make a dandy shot pouch. They would not be spilling their shot all the time. So I cut out a little long buckskin bag and used coarse linen thread to sew it. I had overcast the seam on one side of the bag, gathered it a little at the top and lashed it around the rim of that cartridge shell with the same linen thread.'

"After she was through telling the court all of this they handed her the shot pouch, and sure enough, it was the very same little shot pouch that she had made.

"The attorney turned to Joe and said, 'Young man, what have you to say about that? Sheriff Boyce picked that bag of shot up on Harry Dwyer's root house just outside his back door.'

"That was too much for Joe. That and the fact that he had Dwyer's watch and chain on when he was arrested in Victoria was too much [Author's note: perhaps a misremembering on Mrs. Firth's part]. He broke down and gave up the fight. He made an open confession to all of these terrible deeds.

"He said, 'Yes,' he was the guilty party. There was no use to deny it any longer.

"Then by severe questioning they got him started. He told why he did it—for money. He said he knew Harry had plenty of money, he had just sold his sloop. He told how he and his friend, Indian Jim, sneaked around Harry's field and through the bushes that day to get to the house first. He said they found Mrs. Dwyer sitting on the front porch sewing. Then Joe stationed Indian Jim there to watch her while he went down to the field and shot Harry, which he did by walking right in the furrow. Right up close behind him he got in the good shot. Then he ran up to the house to get Mrs. Dwyer. The Indian had her cornered near the back door where she was begging for her life, Joe said. He shot her once there but did not kill her. So he had to load his gun again then, as the gun was a double barrel shotgun with a ramrod attached underneath the two barrels. In his excitement of loading the gun, he laid the shot pouch down on the root house that was right near him and forgot to pick it up.

"Then he shot her again, after which she walked into the house and tumbled down on the rug beside her bed. She still was not dead. He said he was darn hard to kill, so he beat her over the head with the stock of the gun till he was sure she was dead. He supposed that was how the blood came on the stock of the gun.

"Then the robbery began. I never did hear how much money they found.

"During the trial the sheriff had them ask Joe if he had killed Mr. Fullar a year or more before, and he said yes.

" 'For his money?' 'Yes.'

"Then he told bravely how he planned and completed that murder. He said he and Indian Jim found this large Madrona tree that branched out from the ground where a sheep might get caught. Then Joe hid in the ferns nearby this tree. He sent Jim up to tell Mr. Fullar that he had been hunting and found a sheep of his caught in a big tree down by a fern flat there and he had better come and get it out. So Mr. Fullar went and he led him out near the tree. When Fullar got about to the tree Joe shot him through the head. Then they threw those big rocks on his head and body to be sure of their cruel work. Then they went and robbed his home.

"Among other questions, he was asked if he attended Fullar's funeral. In a very amused way he answered yes—that he wore Fullar's shoes to Fullar's funeral. Joe Nuanna also acknowledged that he had planned to murder Mr. and Mrs. Terrell next, as he thought they had money.

" 'Next,' he said, 'I had planned to kill John and Bill Kady [Keddy],' two bachelor brothers who had a large sheep range near the north end of the Island, on Kady's [Cady] Mountain.' "

On the morning of March 6th, 1874, Joe Nuanna was shown the coffin that would be his eternal resting place. "Why didn't you paint the d—n thing?" he demanded. By ten o'clock, throngs of Port Townsend residents and San Juan Islanders and Klallam Indians had crowded onto the beach below Point Hudson where the gallows had been erected. Nuanna was led up the scaffold by Sheriff Boyce, who was in charge of the proceedings. His hands were in his coat pockets, as he had requested not to be bound as was usually done. Boyce, a compassionate man, had complied. The condemned conferred with a Catholic clergyman for a few minutes before turning to the crowd and removing his kepi hat. He said, "I am very sorry for what I have done; all hands, goodbye." He dropped at five minutes past ten—and what happened next would haunt Sheriff Boyce for the rest of his days.

The stiff noose had shifted under Nuanna's chin, and so his neck was not immediately broken. The slight young man swayed on the rope for thirteen minutes, alive, thrashing and strangling slowly as the life drained from him at an excruciating pace. Boyce had been forced to add his own weight to the rope, and had tried to force the noose back around Nuanna's neck with his boot heel. Finally, after twenty minutes, a doctor pronounced Nuanna dead. The crowd dispersed from the beach, all deeply disturbed by what they had seen, and Sheriff Boyce would never take part in another hanging—in fact, no one was ever hanged in Port Townsend again, or in San Juan County until twenty-one years later. San Juan County, officially incorporated only a few months before, had been inaugurated with one of the most horrifying events in its entire history.

# Roche Harbor and the Hotel de Haro

*We took on gasoline. This place looks interesting, but visitors are not encouraged to look around.*

That was the logbook entry recorded by local writer Lucile S. McDonald in the 1940s, when she and her party briefly docked at Roche Harbor—the bizarre little "fiefdom" at the north end of San Juan Island. From 1887 to 1956, the John S. McMillin family ruled the isolated company town with an iron fist, exerting their influence over everything from politics to local media. As a rather partisan newspaper editor once wrote, "[...] the fountain from which many men draw their political inspiration, and before which they bow as a heathen bows before an idol, bubbles within the shadows of the Roche Harbor lime works." McMillin was the Gilded Age-tycoon of his own diminutive empire, and by most accounts assumed the air of an autocrat—an influence that is still felt well into the present day.

John S. McMillin had first come to the San Juans as a lime prospector in the early 1880s. He had been sent by the Tacoma firm of Henry Cowell, proprietor of a lime empire himself, to inspect the tremendous limestone ledges said to span the peninsula from Roche Harbor to Westcott Bay. First quarried by the Royal Marines of English Camp in 1860, rumors of the fantastically-pure deposit had only recently reached the major lime companies. When McMillin saw these ledges, however, he quickly cast-off all notions of loyalty to Cowell and set about acquiring the land for himself. By 1886, he had done just that.

There had already been a small-time lime operation on the site. The Marines had erected a pair of rudimentary pot kilns at Roche Harbor to burn lime for whitewash-making, mortar, and disinfectant, and had sent samples to Victoria for assaying. It was "[...] a splendid article of lime, white as chalk," reported the *British Colonist*. The British were undoubtedly aware of the lime's enormous potential and guarded it zealously, claiming that it fell within the boundaries of the loosely-defined British military reserve. In November of 1860 yet another international controversy arose when two Americans, Soloman Meyerbach and Paul K. Hubbs, were arrested while skulking around the lime ledges with picks and shovels. Captain George Bazalgette, the Marine commander, had ordered that anyone caught trespassing there was to be detained in the guardhouse, and this was duly done. The Americans protested, eventually leading to a formal defining of the American and British military reserves—as it happened, the Roche Harbor lime fell squarely within the British possession.

When the British left in 1872, a settler named Joseph Ruff was quick to homestead the land and file a mineral claim. Ruff was heavily indebted, however, and was forced to sell after only five years. The buyers were the London-born brothers Robert and Richard Scurr, and the sordid San Juan Town merchant Israel Katz, who acquired the deposit for just one thousand dollars. Katz, perhaps making a rare lapse in judgment, eventually sold out to the Scurrs, and thus abandoned his stake in one of the wealthiest lime deposits in the world.

The Scurr brothers, both veterans of the California goldfields, cleared out one hundred acres for orchards and sheep pasturage—but the great grey marble ridge that loomed up behind the windswept firs was their real focus. By 1879, they were burning lime in the old British kilns and producing crude split-cedar barrels bound with sapling hoops. In 1883, the Scurrs sold a part-interest to the Ross brothers, a trio of Nova Scotians who had worked at the McCurdy kiln at Lime Kiln Point. This partnership would last only until 1885, when both parties elected to sell out to a shadowy buyer named Edward S. Smith—in reality, a front for John S. McMillin. By October of 1886, the entirety of Roche Harbor was openly under McMillin's control as the Tacoma and Roche Harbor Lime Company. The last remnant of the Scurrs' operation, an old bunkhouse, would become the bones of McMillin's opulent new Hotel de Haro.

The arrival of McMillin marked a massive upheaval for the island community. For many years, the only real industry on San Juan had been the ramshackle kilns at Lime Kiln Point and Point Caution, rough-hewn places manned by whiskey-drinkers and other unsavory characters. Now, however, came the era of the company town. McMillin was a man obsessed with order and discipline; there would be no saloons at Roche Harbor, and employees were paid in proprietary company scrip. A high-degree initiate of the Masonic Knights Templar, he cared greatly for ritual and showmanship, as evidenced by his famed Lammas festivals that were once held on the ornamental lawn above the docks. It was the only time of the year that San Juan Islanders were encouraged to visit Roche Harbor, and many were afterwards surprised to receive a bill for the festival's refreshments. A "harvest festival," Mc-Millin's Lammas celebrations were steeped in Masonic mystique and personal whim.

U.S. Customs Service agents had been stationed at Roche Harbor since 1883, well before McMillin's arrival—their assignment was to keep a lookout for smugglers, who often attempted to reach the island from Haro Strait. The agents were none too pleased when McMillin began to establish himself on the lonely bay.

"This is perfect banishment in my case," wrote one customs agent in 1891, "as the 'autocrat' here is displeased with my not reporting everything to him and because I did not work for his ticket on election day, so he makes it as disagreeable as he can for me." The agents were unhappy, too, with McMillin's monopoly over trade in the area. They, like the magnate's employees, were forced to shop at the company store, which charged exorbitant prices for basic goods.

McMillin had his reasons for discouraging interlopers. He had built the Hotel de Haro mainly to house newly-hired employees—a man and his family would stay at the hotel for their first month and run up a hefty bill, leaving them in considerable debt to the company by the time they found superior lodging. Many employees—mainly German, Russian, British, and Japanese immigrants—were brought under McMillin's control in this manner; he had effectively created a serf class for his personal fiefdom. McMillin's bearing was similarly imperious: many recalled McMillin's demand that employees—and even his own children—stand at attention when he entered a room.

The "Lime Baron" soon controlled nearly all aspects of political life on San Juan Island. A prominent Republican Party donor, he purchased influence with the local newspaper and was able to quash controversy with relative ease— such as a letter submitted to the *Seattle Times* that decried McMillin's use of child labor in his staveless barrel factory.

"[...] While we deplore the existing evil [child labor] we have only to visit Roche Harbor, in this state, to see it duplicated. Boys of 7 years of age and upwards work all day long in the barrel factory, and are pitiful specimens of dwarfed childhood," read the letter, signed by the *nom de plume* "Fair Play." The *San Juan Islander*, the local newspaper, responded with a fiery editorial that seemingly doubled-down on the practice, suggesting that while there were children working at the kilns, they were better off at Roche Harbor than they would be elsewhere.

"If there are any 'pitiful specimens of dwarfed childhood' at Roche Harbor, the humanitarian who desires to find the cause will need to look elsewhere than the barrel factory or cooper shop. There are no hard task masters in either place making life a burden for young or old," retorted the *Islander*.

McMillin, meanwhile, ruled from his baronial estate about a mile from the quarry—surrounded by ten-foot steel fencing and an expansive deer park, it was a dramatic locale in which to court the prominent men of the era. One man who would not "kiss the ring," however, was Henry Cowell. The spurned Cowell had bought out several other lime operations in the San Juans simply to "bedevil" his old employee, including the workings at Lime Kiln Point and a number of kilns on Orcas Island. Local sympathies, it seemed, lay largely with Cowell, as McMillin's behavior had hardly endeared him to the islanders. The two competed with each other for years, buying more and more properties to encroach on the other's operations, until finally Cowell was shot in the shoulder over an unrelated boundary dispute in March of 1903. He passed away five months later. His name lives on in the famed Henry Cowell Redwoods State Park in Santa Cruz County, California.

Cowell's son, Ernest, began a series of lawsuits against McMillin two years later, charging his father's old rival with misdeeds ranging from fraud to embezzlement to the withholding of corporate dividends—though the two Lime Barons had been sworn enemies, Cowell had still owned a small amount of stock in the Tacoma and Roche Harbor Lime Company. Another dispute also arose during this time; McMillin had made plans with a Canadian consortium to construct a state-of-the-art Portland cement plant at Roche Harbor, but the Canadians had refused to purchase stock in his company as long as Ernest Cowell still held an interest. Cowell refused to sell out, and the deal was thus blocked; though in June of 1909, the District Court judge ruled in McMillin's favor, saying: "All this fuss has cost me labor in digesting a mass of chaff and straw in order to find a kernel of matter supposed to be contained therein. But there is no kernel."

In the end, Cowell didn't care—as the case festered in the court system, he had built one of the largest cement plants on the West Coast, near Concord, California, and in doing so had defeated John S. McMillin at his own game.

By the 1910s, McMillin had turned over day-to-day management of the company to his eldest son, Fred, and retired to an opulent Mediterranean-style estate called "Afterglow Manor" overlooking Spieden Channel. Fred passed away in 1922, heralding a steady downturn for the Roche Harbor kilns. The staveless barrel factory was destroyed by a fire—allegedly arson—the following year, along with several other structures ranging from wharves to warehouses. "Jap Town," the segregated community where the company's Japanese workers were housed, never recovered. Management of the company was given to the younger son, Paul.

By the early 1930s, McMillin was beginning to anticipate the end; of his own life, and perhaps of the company, as well. He began devising plans for Afterglow Vista, an imposing seven-pillared, Masonic-inspired mausoleum in the nearby woods that would serve as the future resting place for himself and his family. He would be its first interment in November of 1936, having passed away at the age of eighty-one.

The Hotel de Haro closed in 1942, and Afterglow Manor burned on Memorial Day, 1944. Lime was becoming less and less useful in public works projects, and was now mainly quarried for use as "paper rock" in Washington's many paper mills. By the 1950s, Paul McMillin was suffering from various physical ailments, as well as terrible anxiety over the future of the now-struggling company. Roche Harbor was steadily deteriorating, the buildings falling apart and the kilns crumbling, and only forty employees now remained on the payroll. Fortunately for Paul, salvation would come in the form of the Reuben Tarte family of Bellevue.

Tarte and his wife Clara had first visited the San Juans in the 1930s, aboard their yacht the *Clareu II*. They had been surprised to find that, despite the area's wealth of gunkholes and bays and sheltered channels, there was no real boating resort of any kind; or even a safe place to tie up, aside from a few old pilings. The Tartes would remedy this in September of 1956, when they approached McMillin with an undisclosed offer for his four thousand acres and twelve miles of coastline. Tarte had made a fortune with his invention of the now-ubiquitous "piggyback" railroad car, and he now had a vision for a "boater's paradise" on Roche Harbor.

The first order of business was to fulfill the company's remaining lime contracts. This was over-seen largely by Tarte's son Neil and son-in-law Robert Tangney, while simultaneously constructing all-new marina facilities; the rush was on to have the marina completed in time for next year's boating season. Neil Tarte described the experience as akin to being "sent back in time"; the hermit fiefdom was still a strange, sealed-off place, filled with "secretive, eccentric old folks."

By the summer of 1957 the new Roche Harbor marina was open for business, though without food service or other amenities. This would change with the restoration of the ancient Hotel de Haro.

The hotel had been abandoned for nearly twenty years by then, and had taken on a rather foreboding appearance—the roof and verandas were shaggy with moss and lichens and the black windows leered out from behind walls of English ivy. Tales of ghostly knocking, phantom footsteps, and the appearance of a terrifying "wraith" had circulated for years, but did little to deter Clara Tarte and her assistants from tackling the intimidating project. The women cut down the curtains of ivy and repainted the peeling walls, while antique furniture was sourced and drywall hung to replace the moldering plaster. A section of wall was left uncovered by the staircase, revealing the hotel's original hand-quartered log construction; some claimed that the hotel had been built around an 1840s Hudson's Bay Company outpost. This is almost certainly not the case, as the H.B.C. is not known to have built anything larger than a sheep-pen north of Grandma's Cove, some twelve miles to the south. The original log building was likely a bunkhouse built by the Scurr brothers in the early 1880s. Nevertheless, the legend endures.

The Hotel de Haro finally reopened with a grand celebration on New Year's Eve, 1960. Roche Harbor Resort had more or less reached its final form by then—pleasurecraft slips, a gas dock, grocery store, post office, airstrip, restaurant, and other amenities had all been constructed, cementing the resort's position as the premier "boatel" of the San Juans. The hotel, once a "trap" for vulnerable working men and their families, had now joined the likes of Rosario and the Outlook Inn as the archipelago's grand old accommodations.

The Tartes had also stumbled across a rather ghoulish remnant of the old McMillin days while cleaning out the hotel. As Neil Tarte related,

"One morning Paul [McMillin] called me up and said, 'Neil, tomorrow morning I want you to go get the Chrysler, and get a hold of Al Johnson and Cal Morrow, and have them come over and pick up Mrs. Beany and take her to the mausoleum.'

"I had never heard of Mrs. Beany and assumed she was one of the women who worked in the McMillin house, perhaps going up to pay respects to the family.

"When I got a hold of Al and Cal, two of the most trusted McMillin employees, and told them what Paul had said, they both got kind of a blank look on their faces."

According to Tarte, the pair mumbled "Oh, my God . . . oh, dear . . .", and continued in this fashion for over a minute.

"I said, 'what's the problem?' They said, 'Well, she's dead.' I said, 'Where in the world is she?' And they said, 'She's downstairs in a Mason jar on the mantle,' referring to her ashes kept on the fireplace where the bar is now."

"Mrs. Beany" was Ada Beane, the longtime gover-ness of the McMillin children and John's personal secretary, whose life is still shrouded in mystery. She lived next door to the McMillins, in a house that was built identically to the family's. No one knew where she came from; most agreed that she was brought to Roche Harbor as a young girl. Some said she never left the island afterward, or even the McMillin compound. She never married, either—her relation-ship with the Lime Baron was fodder for numerous all-manner of rumors. According to legend, she hanged herself in the upstairs room of her house in 1944.

"They said that Paul and his wife had been talking for two years about taking Mrs. Beany's ashes up and putting them in the family [crypt] with the baby," continued Tarte.

Tarte wanted to know if it was *really* Mrs. Beany's—or Beane's—wish to be sealed up with the McMillins for all of eternity; and so he went to speak with the aged Roche Harbor bookkeeper, Mr. Maggy, a man who seemed to know every strange secret of the old kilns and their crumbling family dynasty.

"So I walked up to the office and I said, 'Mr. Maggy, tell me about Mrs. Beany.' Mr. Maggy, a little short fellow who wore the old green eyeshade and arm bands of a bookkeeper, turned to me and he said, 'Mr. Tarte, let me show you'."

As Maggy explained, "If I remember right, part of

the purchase price of the stock you're buying from Roche Harbor includes a bonded indebtedness of $40,000 that is to be paid directly to Mrs. Paul McMillin'."

"That's right," said Tarte, "that's to be done this March."

Maggy pulled down yellowed and flyspecked ledgers from the sagging shelves, opening each and pointing to entry after entry that showed Mrs. Beane loaning sums of *her own money* to the Roche Harbor Lime & Cement Company—"$500 here, $500 there, $1,000 another time, and so forth." Over the years, Ada Beane had loaned the McMillins around forty thousand dollars.

"Then Maggy showed me an entry in the books indicating that two days before Mrs. Beany's death the entire sum of $40,000 was transferred over to Mrs. McMillin, Paul's wife," said Tarte.

Therefore, the forty thousand dollars that the Tartes would pay to Mrs. Paul McMillin was, in truth, money that the McMillins owed to Ada Beane.

"Ever since that day we put her ashes into the copper urn in the family crypt, she's refused to leave us alone at the resort. Lights go on and off. Doors open and close. The blender turns itself on. The usual ghostly pranks," said Tarte. The ashes had indeed been placed inside John S. McMillin, Jr. 's crypt at Afterglow Vista shortly after their discovery—the child had lived for only two days in 1878.

Reports of a ghostly "wraith" plagued the area for

decades after. Some saw her as a middle-aged woman in a long dress, usually on the hotel's second story, who appeared to be searching for someone—and others reported a "bride in an old-fashioned wedding dress" wandering along Roche Harbor Road in the dead of night. The faint sounds of a crying child were also heard, leading some to suspect that the ghosts were that of Ada Beane and one of the McMillin children, perhaps searching for each other in the dark rooms of the old hotel. But no one could be sure.

Stories of ghostly women, unexplained sounds, and objects moving of their own accord prevailed throughout the 1960s, as workers continued to improve the grounds of the old lime works. One possible explanation was offered by longtime employee Dave Gibbs, who began working at the resort when he was seventeen years old. On a particularly dark and rainy night, he ascended to the then-unused third story of the hotel and began scraping the floor with a stiff brush. His fellow employees on the floor below were so terrified by the "unexplained" sounds that they bolted for the exit. Gibbs's prank, however, fails to account for the physical apparitions often reported.

Gibbs did have "real" ghostly tales of his own, however, after over fifteen years as a restaurant manager in the aged hotel. "Late at night after I've closed up the restaurant and I'm on my way out, I'll look back and a candle will have been reignited. I'll go back to blow out the candle and she'll turn all the hood fans on," said Gibbs.

"She would never hurt you," said giftshop manager Darlene Trobaugh. "But you can feel her presence because Ada lets us know when she is there."

Trobaugh related an incident that befell a shop girl in previous years. The girl was working alone one night, when suddenly, "a multi-layered set of glass shelves started cracking in the middle, falling like dominoes, one on top of the other until shattered shelves and their contents lay scattered over the floor." The girl quit soon after.

Another former gift shop employee had a more detailed account of her experiences at the Hotel de Haro:

"I worked at the gift shop in the main hotel structure in the early 2000s. I heard many stories about [Ada], a mischievous presence who primarily played tricks on those who worked at the hotel. She can be seen at a certain window in the restaurant at times, moving things around, breaking things, etc. One late fall afternoon, I had been folding all the shirts, sweaters, shorts, sweatshirts in the back room of the gift shop for nearly an hour, arranging dozens of piles to look 'just so'. No one had been in for over two hours. I went to the closed door to look out, trying to decide if I should close early. Not seeing anyone, I turned back to the back room. The first item of clothing on each stack looked like someone had picked it up, shaken it out, wadded it up, and stuffed it back into place. This had happened to roughly 4 dozen items of clothing in less than 10 seconds. While I stood there in the doorway, mouth open, I felt an icy draft pass over me, causing all my hairs to stand up. They do that every time I tell this story.

"Ten years later I went back to look around. I spoke to the new sales person in the shop, asking cautiously if she had experienced anything 'strange' while working there. She narrowed her eyes and asked what I meant. Shrugging, I told her about my experiences and stories from old co-workers. She loudly exclaimed 'Oh thank God, I thought I was going crazy!' and proceeded to tell me about things that seemed to be happening overnight in locked storage rooms, papers shifting, stacks moving.

"For the past 15 years, whenever I learn that someone had worked there (and in such a small community, easily 40% of Islanders have at some point in their lives) I ask if they ever experienced something unexplainable. At this point, over 60% have had stories of their own to tell.

"Also, I have been told of a few would-be guests who have refused to go up the stairs to their rooms, saying that there was something evil up there. Some suspect a second, not-so-harmless presence."

Many of the legends surrounding Ada Beane were just that; it was variously reported that she had been John S. McMillin's mistress, and had hanged herself after becoming pregnant, or that she had died of natural causes before the child was born. Regardless, there is nothing to support these lurid claims. At least one disturbing incident really *did* take place in the Hotel de Haro, however; a 1985 murder-suicide to rival the horror of the Kanaka Joe killings, though one that has been comparatively forgotten today.

Twenty-five-year-old Marilyn Hamilton, formerly of Moscow, Idaho, had worked as a clerk at the Roche Harbor grocery store for two years. She had been seeing a young marine machinist named John Lovegren at the time of the killings. Only a day before, Marilyn had left her long-term boyfriend, a five-times-divorced Friday Harbor businessman named Richard "Dick" Nelson—a man nearly twenty-five years her senior. Hamilton had left Moscow to live with Nelson, it was later revealed.

"He was divorced and already had kids," recalled a front desk clerk. "She wanted to raise a family. That was one of the reasons she wanted to leave him."

Lovegren was described as "a real boat lover and really dear friend." He had helped Clyde and Betty Rice sail their large yacht up from Portland two years before, which the Rices had operated as a floating bed-and-breakfast in Friday Harbor.

"Until he met Marilyn, boats were the only thing that meant anything to him," said Clyde. "He was a typical young sailing type: quiet, shy, not very effusive, a private person. John had been very cautiously looking for a lady for some time. He knew Marilyn at Roche Harbor for the full summer, but it wasn't until Christmas that their relationship blossomed into a bubbling, joyous affair—the kind we cherish in our hearts. He was going to sell his boat and get the money for a 'nest' for them."

Nelson had other plans for the young couple. His behavior had become increasingly deranged—he began harassing Hamilton with threats of violence and self-harm in the weeks leading up to the murders. "When she got unhappy, he would get out a gun and threaten suicide," said a friend of Hamilton. Nelson's threats were hardly hollow, as it happened.

"When she told Dick she was moving out, he forced her to stay," said the friend. "Early last week he pulled a gun […] she stayed because he wouldn't let her out of the house. But then he went to Seattle and she went to work. John met her at the Roche Harbor store on Tuesday. Dick showed up there and threatened her with the gun. John said he told Dick to go ahead and shoot. Instead, Dick ended up with tears in his eyes, shaking Dick's hand."

The day after Hamilton finally left him for good, however, Nelson "worked himself into a frenzy" and drove to the Hotel de Haro. Hamilton and Lovegren were together when Nelson arrived at around 10:30 on the morning of January 10th, 1985. He broke down the door and shot Lovegren twice at close range with a 9mm, while Hamilton managed to grab a telephone and dial the hotel's switchboard. The operator heard the third gun-shot and dispatched security guards to the room —but by then it was too late. Lovegren and Hamilton were dead, and Nelson had turned the pistol on himself. The room was splattered with blood and viscera from floor to ceiling.

The room was never rented again. Used as storage, many continued to hear strange knocks and footsteps coming from inside the "Murder Room," as it came to be called, even when it was locked up and empty.

"We had a guest complain about someone thumping around a lot and making a lot of noise in the next room," said former front desk clerk Pete Hayes*. "I asked what their room number was, and they told me [...] and right away I got kind of a sinking feeling in my stomach. Then I asked them if it was from the room on their left or right. When they said right, I knew they were talking about the Murder Room. I think we just switched them to a different room and didn't talk about it any more than that. We never put anyone next to the Murder Room for that reason, when we could help it."

Perhaps the most spine-tingling reminder of the 1985 murders was a late-night phone call received by one of Pete's fellow clerks.

"My supervisor at the time used to work the front desk in the late eighties," recalled Pete. "She told me that, a few years after the murders, she'd been dozing off a little bit when the phone rang. She picked it up without thinking, and on the other end she heard a woman scream '*help me*,' and then what sounded like a gunshot. And then the line went dead. It turned out the call had come from the Murder Room, which was still listed on the switchboard—but the phone had been disconnected a long time before."

The ghostly happenings at Roche Harbor are hardly confined to the Hotel de Haro. Unusual activity has been reported on the site of the old Jap Town village on Bazalgette Point, just south of the main resort—an area that was developed into condominiums in the mid-1970s. Jap Town had once housed the lime company's sizable Japanese population, many of whom worked as powdermen and domestic help at the McMillin estate and hotel. Large numbers of illegal Japanese immigrants had also been smuggled through the area, likely with the company's tacit approval; illegal workers were often employed at the kilns, as the era's loose labor laws certainly did not apply to them, nor did wage standards. A prominent scandal had occurred in 1901, when customs agents arrested a total of twenty-four Japanese nationals at Roche Harbor, and at a logging camp on Waldron Island; most had been employed as contract woodcutters for the Mc-Millin kilns. "Jim the Gardener," a Japanese man personally employed by McMillin, had recruited the illegals in British Columbia. Despite all this, the Lime Baron himself was never implicated.

At least two graves at the Roche Harbor Cemetery are marked entirely in kanji; another is that of a quarryman named Y. Ohno, who was killed in a dynamite explosion. An unknown number of unmarked graves surround the crumbling stones, many of them likely Japanese, according to local historians.

Pat and Diane Ramseur rented one of the Bazalgette Point condominiums in the early 1990s: "We were building our house at Yacht Haven at the time, and we needed somewhere to stay," says Pat. "We'd already sold our place in Huntington Beach, and one of these condos at Roche came up on the market. Very nice place [...] had about fourteen hundred square feet, and a boat slip and everything. Almost put our house now to shame!"

During their eight months or so at the "Jap Town" condominium, the Ramseurs reportedly experienced a variety of strange occurrences.

"I've never been one for ghosts, but Diane just loves them," says Pat. "That being said, I had a few encounters that left me wondering. I remember one night, Diane went to one of her mahjong games that she used to have with her friends, and I was left home alone for a few hours. So I camped out in the living room and started flipping through channels. Well, after maybe an hour I got up to get a can of Coke or something like that, and as I got up I looked out the sliding glass door that faced out towards the forest next to the house [...] and I just about had a heart attack, because there was a man standing at the door, in the dark, about an inch away from the glass. Now, it was pitch black outside, but I could clearly see an Oriental man's face, even though there was a lot of reflection from inside the house there. He was a pale-skinned looking guy, pasty, and staring right at me without any kind of expression. I was pretty much speechless, I think, but right as I was about to yell out, you know, 'and just *who* are you?', I blinked—and he was gone. Just plain gone. I ran over and flipped on the porch light, and I went outside and checked things out, but there wasn't any sign of anyone. No twigs snapping or nothing. He was just gone, like he'd been on the TV and I changed the channel. I remember very distinctly, though, seeing his breath on the glass after he'd gone. It was almost frosty, which was strange because it was a warm summer night at the time.

"We had a few other things happen, sure. Things would go missing and then reappear elsewhere, things like that. A friend of ours used to joke that we had a carbon monoxide leak [...] Diane was the most 'sensitive,' though. She's always going in for ghost tours and those paranormal hunter TV shows. To this day she says that condo was haunted by the spirits of the Japanese people who'd lived there at the turn of the century. Maybe she got the idea from me, after I told her about the guy I saw! But, I don't know. I know she used to find little pieces of broken china and glass and things when she was digging in her flowerbeds. Leftovers from the Jap Town that used to be there, probably."

There had been around twenty cottages on the site of the present-day Lagoon Park and West Point Condominiums until the 1923 fire. Not all of the dwellings had been affected, but the population nevertheless declined steadily afterwards, until the last

Japanese family left Roche Harbor in 1932. Diphtheria outbreaks and fatal mishaps in the quarries had taken the rest.

Perhaps the strangest ghostly tale to originate at Roche Harbor comes from Port Orchard yachtsman Greg Pollard, a regular attendee of the annual Tollycraft Rendezvous with his wife Trudy.

"In the summer of 2004, Johnny Carson—he was the host of the old Tonight Show, for all [the] kids who don't know anyone past Leno—spent the summer cruising around the San Juans on his big tri-deck Westport. Big, hundred and thirty-foot yacht. He was based out of Roche Harbor for most of that time, and when Trudy and I came up from Orchard about a week before the Rendezvous, we were there at the same time as Johnny. Now, I think he must have had a chef on board, but we'd see him at McMillin's [restaurant] and at the store once in a while. When I met him the first time, I remember I was leaning over the side of the dock, looking down at some little minnows or something, I think, when someone walked up behind me and tapped me on the shoulder, and said 'Hello, I'm Johnny!' Now, it took me a second to register it, because I'd heard those words a million times on the Tonight Show, but when I turned around, d—ned if it wasn't Johnny Carson!

"Of course, Johnny was a lot older then, and he'd been struggling with emphysema for a few years. But he was just as chatty as ever, and he wanted to know if I'd done any fishing off the docks. I said I hadn't, but a buddy of mine had hooked a pretty good-sized humpy right off the end of the dock one time, and that, '04 being a pink year, he should cruise over to Kellett Bluff and try around there. He said he'd try it out, but looking back on it he was probably just being polite.

"We got to talking, and he told me about how happy he was to have found the San Juans, that he hadn't been up there much before. Or maybe he hadn't ever, I don't remember. John Wayne had told him about the islands, he said. [Wayne] used to stay at Roche Harbor all the time when he had the *Wild Goose*. We talked about all kinds of stuff [...] he said my Tollycraft was a heck of a boat, and I said, 'well, it looks like a washtub compared to yours!' He had a superyacht, after all. He said, 'well, it's a money pit,' and some-times it felt less personal, maybe, cruising on a big giant yacht like that. It felt more like a cruise ship, sometimes, than his own boat. He said, I remember, 'Greg, there's times I would trade it all for a little cabin cruiser, a tide chart, and a good woman at my side—and leave the personal chef and boatswain's mate and all that on the dock!' And coming from a guy like Johnny Carson, I think that was the best compliment I could have ever asked for.

"Well, just a few months after that, it was all over the news that Johnny had passed away. He'd struggled with illness for a long time—he told me he'd smoked four packs a day for thirty or forty years. And that just caught up with him. But it was still kind of a shock, since I'd only talked to him a few months before. Anyways, we had the Rendezvous again that June, 2005, and like before we got there a week or so beforehand. Late one evening, I went out to the dock, just on a little walk while Trudy was fixing dinner. I ended up in about the same spot where I'd run into Johnny the year before, and I just stood there and watched the sun going down over Henry Island. No sunsets like that anywhere else in the world, they're just the most beautiful thing you've ever seen. And as I was standing there, I felt a little cool breeze kind of brush past me, and clear as day I felt a hand on my shoulder—and a voice said, 'Hello, I'm Johnny!' Well, you can imagine how I felt when I turned around and there was nobody there!

"I think, looking back, it was Johnny's spirit, come to say hello to an old acquaintance. He'd told me how much he loved the San Juans, and Roche Harbor, and even if he'd only been able to enjoy them for a few months before he passed, that was the place he'd always wanted to call home."

Though many of the old structures and kilns remain, the character of Roche Harbor today is dramatically different from that of the old McMillin days. Gone are the child laborers in the barrel factory, and the Lammas rituals, and the strange secrecy that once dominated the place—replaced with a cheerful and recreational air that few other resorts can rival. Today, the last remains of the odd old days are found in the crumbling kilns, beneath the condominiums on

Bazalgette Point, and wandering the dark hallways of the Hotel de Haro . . .

# Afterglow Vista

In a way, the limestone itself is a tomb—the rock is a hardened mass of fossilized and fused-together organisms and pieces of shell and coral from long-vanished seas. Laborers in the San Juan quarries would occasionally excavate bizarre fossils entombed deep in the stone, but no particular value was placed on such things. Their crushed remnants now lie deep beneath the city streets of Seattle and Portland and even far-flung Honolulu.

As he entered his twilight years, the Lime Baron John S. McMillin began devising plans for a spectacular monument to himself and his family. Sitting near remains of the old Afterglow Manor estate, which burned in 1944, Afterglow Vista was a *tholos*—a broad circle of cement and limestone from which rose seven Tuscan columns, one of them symbolically broken to represent the "unfinished state of man's work when the string of life is broken." The entirety of the mausoleum is steeped in Masonic symbolism, much like the life of the man who built it. McMillin was a high-degree member of the Knights Templar sect of Freemasonry, and his epitaph reflected this lofty and ritual-minded outlook: JOHN STAFFORD McMILLIN, A.B., A.M., LL.D. - A 32° MASON - KNIGHT TEMPLAR - NOBLE OF MYSTIC SHRINE ΣX - METHODIST - REPUBLICAN. A list of beliefs inscribed, perhaps, in order of personal importance.

In the center of the tholos sits a stone table, altarlike, surrounded by six cast-cement chairs inscribed with the names of departed McMillins—their cremated remains are contained in the crypts below. The chairs are spaced equally around the table, aside from one notable gap that corresponds to a missing chair, in-line with the broken column; a gap that has kindled the imaginations of countless visitors over the years. Some said the missing chair and column represented a "black sheep" of the family, usually identified as Paul McMillin, who had apparently rejected the Masonic ways of his father and older brother. In truth, the gap allows in a ray of the setting sun that strikes the seats of John S. McMillin and his wife during the vernal equinox and "completes" the column—the "afterglow" of the sunset over Haro Strait, once the McMillins' dinnertime view, washes over the barestone columns and causes them to flame red and pink and take on the color of the madronas that surround the tomb. A visitor once described the sight as reminiscent of some forgotten forest-temple to Circe or Dionysus or the shadowy Pan—"like something out of Tolkien or Arthur Machen," he said.

The steps leading up the rocky slope to the mausoleum are themselves symbolic of the mysterious Masonic tenets. Divided into three tiers, the riser of the first is inscribed McMILLIN, and contains three steps. The second tier has five, and the third seven; allegedly denoting the three stages of manhood, the five senses and five orders of architecture, and the seven liberal arts and sciences. Even the meandering pathway from the Roche Harbor Cemetery that winds and twists through the dark woods represents "how the future cannot be seen." The fluted columns, meanwhile, are carved to the exact measurements of those found in Solomon's Temple—the supposed origin of Freemasonry itself. According to Masonic belief, the original Masons were the builders of the Temple, and had constructed secret chambers with which to secretly observe the arcane rites performed by the Hebrew high priests within. These discovered mysteries would become the foundation of the Masonic order.

John S. McMillin was no stranger to these tales, as reflected by his high-degree status; and some contend that this belief inspired more than the simply superficial similarities to Solomon's Temple. One wild claim states that, during the mausoleum's six-year construction, the Lime Baron had hired only illegal, non-English speaking laborers to excavate the foundation; the reason being that an elaborate and highly secretive "catacombs" had been dug below the rotunda, accessible only through a well-hidden entrance. The laborers had been summarily deported upon completion to further guard the secret—they had all disappeared, at any rate. Naturally, this tale fails to hold water.

In light of the strange symbology and forbidding figure of the towering, moss-covered mausoleum, many ghostly tales have sprung up around the site. Most follow a similar vein: that on certain nights, wanderers at the moonlit rotunda may sometimes witness mysterious orbs of blue light hovering over the six seats of the limestone table—perhaps the McMillins, gathered once more to share a phantom dinner near the site of their long-vanished estate. Some have reported, too, that on these nights the second-growth forest surrounding Afterglow is strangely absent, and that the panoramic view of the starlit strait is fully visible, as it would have been at the time of the mausoleum's construction.

Others have told of standing within the colonnade on drizzly days, but staying inexplicably dry of the raindrops falling just outside—despite there being no roof on the rotunda. John S. McMillin had supposedly intended to cap the mausoleum with a tremendous bronze dome, an elaborate piece to be surmounted with a massive Maltese cross. However, his son Paul, who had managed the family finances for over a decade, vetoed the idea, citing the extravagant cost of such a vault. This supposed spurning was allegedly another impetus for the broken column motif.

Disembodied voices, cold spots, and phantom hands have also been reported. Visitors who sit in the sepulchral seats find themselves pushed away by an unseen force—or, at the very least, feel a deep sense of unease, and the urge to leave as quickly as possible. Becca Foust, who visited Afterglow Vista in 2019, had this spine-tingling encounter to relate:

"The walk through the cemetery was spooky enough on its own. Lots of graves, a lot of them really overgrown and enclosed in these weird cages. Then the trail just kind of winds through the forest and it's so weird, you kind of lose your sense of time and direction and just go where it takes you and *boom*, it's right there, the mausoleum. It's such an eerie place, like it's right out of a fantasy novel or something. My partner and I were there around twilight, and that made it so much creepier. The forest there gets darker and darker and the mausoleum doesn't. It gets lighter, almost, like it's glowing. I guess it's just that the stone reflects light super well, but I don't know [...] it gives you this feeling of awe and dread all at the same time. Like you want to run away as fast as you can, but you can't at the same time [...] like something is up there in those ruins that's inviting you to climb up those steps and come inside the circle. Something not quite evil, maybe, but something not quite sane either, is what my partner said.

"But, obviously, we went up and walked inside and went up to the table and chairs. Standing in that circle is the weirdest feeling I've ever had. I know what it means to feel like you're being watched. I had an experience with a stalker when I was in college, and I learned what these deep, instinctual kinds of feelings mean and how to interpret them. So [...] standing on that platform, in the middle of those columns, felt like I was on the slide of a microscope. I got this feeling, this sense, like a vision or something, of a huge eyeball staring down at us from the stars, looking right through that circle like a lens and *looking right at me*.

"Then, thank god, my partner finally grabbed my arm and said, 'let's get back to the car, it's getting dark.' As soon as I stepped outside of the columns, I felt I was free again. This weight lifted from my shoulders, and without even looking at each other or saying anything we started taking two or three steps at a time going down, and pretty much ran all the way back to the parking lot. And we didn't talk about it for a long time. Now, you can laugh at this, but it wasn't until we smoked a little bit and kind of got ourselves re-centered and grounded again that we were able to talk about it. My partner had had the exact same feeling that I had. We've never been back there, and I actually tell people, like friends who're visiting, *not* to go there, because [...] I just think there are some things out there that are so beyond what we can even imagine that it's insane to even try to reconcile with that. That we should avoid places like that if we can. The world's big enough that we can do that."

Afterglow Vista, though appearing like a ruin, still holds a prominent place in island life. The Masons of the San Juan Lodge continue to hold their secretive ceremonies among the sacred columns each spring, and tourists flock there throughout the year, most unaware of the strange symbols and their arcane meanings as they wander through the ruins of Lime Baron's life.

# Massacre House

"I've never seen a more haunted house in ten years of doing this," says ghost hunter Randall Maier. "There's something on that land that's unlike anything we've ever seen. I've lived in haunted houses, I grew up in one, and I'm fascinated with them [...] but the [Massacre House] is somewhere that I really would never want to set foot again."

In 2018, Maier and his ghost-hunting group, Bellingham Paranormal Investigations, were contacted by San Juan Island homeowners Tim and Shirley Bunson*. The couple had recently purchased a newly-built home just south of Friday Harbor—the exact location has not been disclosed—and had been living in a state of absolute terror ever since. "Something" else was inhabiting the house, and for the Bunsons, life at their island getaway was quickly becoming a living hell.

"We were looking forward to getting out of the

rat-race," says Tim. "We had scrimped and saved for years so we could buy a place on San Juan. We'd fallen in love with the islands about twenty years ago, and we'd had plans to buy a place for the summer that we could also rent out over the winter. But things started going wrong right away."

The house had been constructed only a year or so before. Located in a wooded area near the old Bald Hill gravel quarry, the land itself had been largely untouched since the pioneer days. "It was a beautiful area," says Tim. "Would have been nicer if it was closer to the water, but no complaints otherwise."

Things took a turn for the bizarre, however, only a few days after moving in.

"It sounded like a herd of elephants on the roof," recalls Shirley. "Maybe that's an exaggeration. But there was someone or something in the attic stomping around and making a huge amount of noise. It woke Tim and I up around midnight and it felt like the whole house was coming down!"

Tim grabbed his nearest available weapon—a bedside lamp—and crept to the small attic trapdoor in the bedroom closet, prepared to ascend and confront the noisemaker above.

"But something stopped me," says Tim. "This wave of fear hit me, and I just knew, in the pit of my stomach, that if I went up there I wouldn't come down."

The terrifying racket abruptly stopped as dawn approached—the Bunsons had laid awake throughout the night, terrified to even leave the bedroom.

"I finally got up the nerve to take a look when the noise had been over for a few hours," says Tim. "I popped my head up [into the attic] and there was nothing out of the ordinary. There were only a few boxes up there and nowhere to hide, really. With the amount of noise we'd heard, I was expecting to see insulation ripped out and stuff thrown around [...] there wasn't anything out of place. There wasn't even room for someone to stand upright, to make the kind of noise we'd heard."

For the next few months, sleep became a rare luxury for the Bunsons. Nearly every night, the same raucous stomping and pounding would occur in the narrow attic, sometimes shaking the entire house with enough force to knock loose vases and framed pictures. Other "manifestations" began to occur, as well—whispered conversations overheard through the walls, mysterious flashes of multi-colored light, and objects disappearing at random all became common-place.

"I had a motion-sensing floodlight in the backyard that would turn on and off so much I finally took it down," says Tim. "It was getting annoying."

By the end of the third month, the Bunsons had had enough.

"We weren't quite ready to accept that there was something paranormal going on," says Shirley. "And we're not bible-thumpers, either. So, I started looking for an investigator of some kind who could help figure out what was going on, while also staying grounded and not too 'woo-woo.' A name that kept coming up was Bellingham Paranormal Investigations—I was a little hesitant to call them at first, mainly because of the 'paranormal' part, but finally, after a really bad night, we decided to anyway [...] it ended up being the best decision we could have made."

Randall Maier and his "team" had already investigated a series of locales in the San Juans the previous year, including the Orcas Hotel and the alleged activity in downtown Eastsound. According to Maier, he and his group "jumped at the chance" to return.

"The islands are an incredibly unique place," says Maier. "People ask what makes them so special, and I always say, 'limestone, limestone, limestone.' Limestone is an incredibly potent mineral that conducts psychic energy in huge volumes, and the San Juans are basically made of limestone. That's also why places like the UK and Appalachia are so famously haunted."

In October of 2018, Maier and three others arrived at the Bunsons' home for a four-day "study." The ghost hunters had brought along all-manner of specialized equipment, including EMF readers, EVP recorders, a full-spectrum camera—and a "real life" medium.

"Our medium, or sensitive person, is a wonderful human being named Wren," says Maier. "She has an incredible ability to sense and to connect with spirits, even those spirits that don't want to be contacted.

She's almost more like a therapist. In one house that we investigated in Happy Valley, a spirit of a man who'd died there refused to let anyone else live there [...] but Wren, in her compassionate and understanding way, was able to convince this spirit to move on, and the house was totally peaceful after that."

Their study would not be so straightforward, however. According to Maier, the presence in the house was so "malignant" that they very nearly reconsidered their commitment as they approached down the driveway.

"You could feel it all around, in the trees, in the grass, in the shadows—and that was before we even saw the house," says Maier. "I actually stopped the van, and I said, 'hey, everyone, I know we're all feeling this right now [...] if anyone wants to turn back right now, no harm no foul. We'll go back to the ferry and forget this ever happened.' But we all agreed that we needed to see it through."

The Bunsons were tremendously relieved when the ghost hunters arrived. "It was like seeing a light at the end of the tunnel," according to Shirley. "Someone to share our experience and tell us, 'no, you're not going crazy, after all'."

At the time, Bellingham Paranormal Investigations had been in talks with the Travel Channel to possibly develop a reality series based on their adventures. Maier and his team viewed the Bunsons' home as a potential filming location for their pilot episode.

"It would have been perfect," says Maier. "So we

wanted to get a feel for what we were dealing with, get some evidence, and then basically approach the studio with what we had and say, 'look, this has the potential to be the next Amityville. Greenlight us!'"

Inside the house, Wren began to experience much of the same phenomena that had been reported by the Bunsons—and even gained a psychic "impression" of the spirits that inhabited the home.

"[Wren] said there were five spirits in the house, and their bodies were buried somewhere close by on the property, maybe even under the house itself. The spirits were Native American warriors, and they app- eared as wearing these really terrifying masks—she's also an amazing artist, and she drew a picture of what she'd seen. Some of these masks looked like human faces with insane makeup and these terrifying facial expressions, and the other ones were more like animal masks. Wolves, ravens, things like that. A little Google-fu told us that these were actually from the Native American communities in Alaska. Wren saw glimpses of these spirits in different rooms in the house, and said they were *not* friendly; they were territorial, and they were angry that a house was built over their resting place. So, of course they blamed the Bunsons for that."

Realizing the need to research the history of the land itself, Maier and his team reached out to the San Juan Island Historical Society for assistance. The story they uncovered—to which they attributed the supp- osed haunting—was a chilling one.

In 1938, a pair of elderly strangers visited the old *Friday Harbor Journal* office and spun a spine-tingling tale to editor Virgil Frits. According to the visitors, they were relatives of the early settler Matthias Rethlefsen, who had settled on Bald Hill in the early 1860s. Rethlefsen was a farmer, and often joked that Bald Hill must have been made of pure gravel, with the amount of small fieldstones that choked his plow. His neighbor was "Uncle" Jack Montgomery, "a man then in his sixties, less than five feet in height, weighing not one hundred pounds; but a man with a quick temper and a trigger-finger to match," according to historian David Richardson.

One fateful day, Uncle Jack spotted an unknown Indian spying through his cabin window. On remote San Juan Island, where Indian attacks by northern war parties still occurred with semi-regularity, such visitations were rarely friendly—and so Montgomery grabbed his rifle and attempted to fire on the man. His weapon misfired two or three times, however, and by the time he had affixed a new cap the interloper had since vanished into the trees. Soon after, Uncle Jack learned that the Indian had been friendly—he had only been attempting to spread the word that a northern war party had been seen in the area.

A few days later, Uncle Jack returned from a hunting trip to find five northern Indians digging up his potato patch. The men had ransacked the cabin and made packs of Jack's blankets to carry valuables, and were then in the process of dividing up his winter spud supply for the journey home. Uncle Jack Montgomery wouldn't be caught off-guard again—he shouldered his rifle and dropped the largest of the five.

The remaining marauders made a mad-dash for the beach, exchanging fire with Montgomery and managing to wound the settler before launching their war canoe and escaping into Griffin Bay. Briefly euphoric at having fought off the raiders, he soon came to the terrifying realization that the escaping Indians would soon be back—and that his scalp would soon decorate some faraway longhouse, alongside that of Colonel Ebey. Knowing that he had little choice, he again raised his rifle and methodically picked off the remaining members of the war party until the canoe drifted aimlessly in the bay. Uncle Jack then rushed to the home of his neighbor, Rethlefsen, and warned that he'd better clear out, because *any* white man's scalp would suffice when the northern Indians were on the warpath.

Rethlefsen had no intention of leaving, however, and managed to soothe the panicked Montgomery. The two trekked down to the beach and saw that the tide had brought in the canoe and its ghastly contents; they carried the bodies inland and buried them beneath a grove of cedars, and then burned the canoe on the beach. When the kinsmen of the slain warriors passed through in search of answers, they found no trace of the vanished party, and left the islands in peace—Uncle Jack's scalp intact.

The old folks who visited Virgil Frits at the newspaper office said that they intended to go out the following day in search of the graves. The next afternoon, they appeared again and said that "in all the years [they] had been away, the woods had reclaimed the field and that the second growth was so dense [they] could scarcely believe they once had a cleared field." The relatives *had* found the graves, however—and to prove it, they produced an old grain bag and rolled a pair of skulls onto the editor's desk.

Bald Hill, the closest landmark to the scene of the killings, was indeed made of gravel. The three hundred-foot ridge was quarried extensively beginning in the 1920s, and has since been reduced to nearly nothing—today it is the Lafarge Open Space park, adjoining the aptly-named Missing Mountain Road.

"It's always a shock when history lines up with a haunting," says Maier. "Reading about this historical massacre of Native Americans and their potential burial on the property [...] it makes your blood run cold. These materials we found at the museum basically confirmed everything we'd experienced so far, and when things like that happen [...] it's humbling."

Armed with this newfound knowledge, the Bellingham Paranormal Investigations crew returned to the Bunson house and set about confronting the issue. Maier continues:

"We sat at the kitchen table and made a conscious effort to contact the spirits. We wanted to communicate that they were heard, they were seen, and they were respected in this space. We played some traditional Native American music, from what we believed to be the spirits' tribe, and basically did everything we could to show that we cared, that they had no reason to feel marginalized."

Things didn't go as planned. Wren, the medium, was seized with a feeling that something was "entering her body," and promptly fell out of her chair and began flailing on the kitchen floor. Meanwhile, the electromagnetic frequency (EMF) readers placed around the room began to wail as an "extremely powerful force" manifested itself, according to Maier.

"We were horrified," says Tim. "We thought [Wren] was having a seizure, and we were about to call 9-1-1, but Randall stopped us and said, 'hold off on that. Let's try something first'."

Maier began performing an impromptu "smudging ritual"—an ancient Indian ceremony where sage or cedar or a similar herb is burned in a bundle, and the fragrant smoke used to cleanse a spiritually-afflicted person or place.

"It was the craziest thing I've ever done," says Maier. "We weren't at all prepared, and I didn't have any sage, which is what's most commonly used. Luckily, I'd read that lavender is a good substitute, and [Shirley] happened to have a potpourri bowl out as decoration. So I grabbed it and threw in a match [...] and thank gods the flame took. I started fanning the smoke over Wren and repeating a verbal request for the spirits to leave. I did this for a while, over five minutes, until Wren calmed down. There was a really palpable sense of relief in the whole room, like this presence had left and everyone knew it. I asked if she was okay, and she said yes, but that she'd like to leave now. So, unfortunately, we had to cut our investingation short by a couple of days. Tim and Shirley were incredibly understanding and compassionate the whole time.

"We gave [Wren] a few days to recuperate, obviously, and then we had a meeting over drinks at the Waterfront Tavern, which is this incredibly spooky dive in Bellingham that we find ourselves coming back to. None of us had looked at any of the data we'd collected yet, we'd just kind of scattered after getting back, and none of us had talked about it since then. I think there was kind of an unspoken agreement that we'd all look at the full-spectrum images and everything together. I brought my laptop to the bar and we looked at the images that were automatically recorded while the encounter was going on. We were absolutely blown away. There were orbs, streaks of light, all kinds of incredible phenomena. But I think, most shockingly, was that in one of the pictures you can clearly see at least three human shapes standing over Wren in the kitchen. They're extremely distorted, but it does appear that the figures are wearing masks, just like how Wren described in her psychic impression. One of them has what looks like wolf ears and a long snout."

The ghostly disturbances *did* abate for the Bunsons, at least for a little while. Though the late-night stomping had ceased, there were a few isolated incidents of flickering lights and random knocks in empty rooms. It was enough for the Bunsons to find a new home elsewhere, this time off-island.

"We gave it our best shot, but we could never feel comfortable living there," says Shirley.

Randall Maier and Bellingham Paranormal Investigations never returned to the Bunson home, but did send the couple a written list of suggestions. The first was to have a qualified Indian shaman purify the land—and the next, to search for the remains and have them respectfully reinterred. The Bunsons followed through, and dutifully contacted a member of the Mitchell Bay Band to conduct a more thorough cedar-smudging ceremony. Afterward, a local psychic aided in a search for human remains on the property—none were found. As of this writing, the Bunsons still own the home near the missing moun-tain, which they now operate as a full-time rental.

"We warn people before they put any money down," says Tim. "But most people don't believe in ghosts. The place has gotten a lot better, but I'll say this—after a week or two at the house, a lot of people change their minds."

As for Maier and his team: "We're totally game to go back. We're still looking at potential studios to produce a reality series, and when that happens, [the Bunson house] will be the pilot. Or the finale. Either way, it's at the top of the list."

*A view of the infamous San Juan Town as illustrated by James Madison Alden, c. 1859. The village was long shunned by decent citizens, and most were pleased to see it burn in 1890.*
(San Juan Island Historical Society collection)

*The abandoned cemetery at American Camp as it appeared c. 1910. Many believe that the graves there were never reinterred.*
(University of Washington collection)

*Belle Vue was the Hudson's Bay Company's lonely and wolf-stalked outpost on San Juan. Today, the area is rife with tales of bizarre activity— including supernatural sea wolves.*
(University of Washington collection)

*American Camp during its heyday, as depicted by artist Richard Schlecht. Life for enlisted men was far from idyllic, however, and soldiers sometimes vanished without a trace.*
(National Park Service collection)

*Mary Crook Davis at English Camp, c. 1950s. The eccentric Crook siblings lived at the dilapidated site for many years.*
(National Park Service collection)

*The English Camp cemetery was the resting place of several Marines who met untimely ends at the lonely cantonment . . . and the scene of at least one ghostly encounter.*
(Emilia Bave collection)

*The ramshackle village at Kanaka Bay as it appeared in the 1870s. This remote fishing outpost was the home of "Kanaka Joe" Nuanna, the infamous mass murderer.*
(San Juan Island Historical Society collection)

*Bald Hill once towered above the Rethlefsen and "Uncle Jack" Montgomery homesteads near North Bay; today, after decades of quarrying, it is known as the "missing mountain."*
(San Juan Island Historical Society collection)

*The Hotel de Haro at Roche Harbor, c. 1959. The storied hotel has been the scene of murder, mayhem, and intrigue for years, and is said to be one of the more haunted locales in Washington state. A phantasmic streak in this photograph may attest to this status.*
*(Seattle Times collection)*

*Deputies remove one of the victims from the Hotel de Haro, c. 1985.*
*Things were never the same at Roche Harbor again.*
*(Journal of the San Juans* collection)

*John S. McMillin's Afterglow Vista mausoleum, c. 1948. The*
*mausoleum has long been fodder for spooky island tales.*
(San Juan Island Historical Society collection)

*"Circle Trigon" troops simulated the enemy during Operation Sea Wall in
1961. These men experienced a variety of strange activity during their stay
on San Juan.*
(22nd Infantry Regiment collection)

*Army personnel and civilians observe infantrymen landing on South Beach
during Operation Sea Wall. The island hadn't seen such a high level of
military hubbub since the Pig War.*
(San Juan Island Historical Society collection)

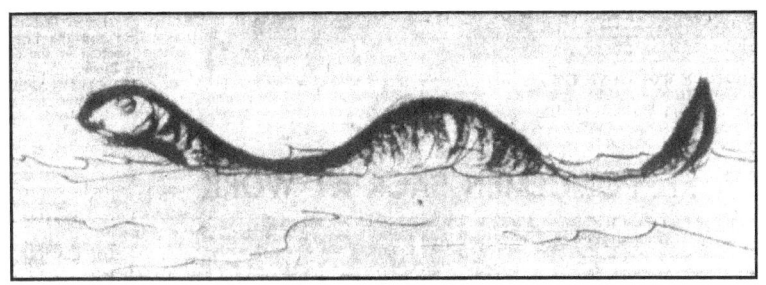

*The famed sea serpent* Cadborosaurus *is said to inhabit the waters of Haro Strait; Caddy's offspring "Fidele," named by Victoria residents in 1969, is pictured above.*
(*Victoria Daily Times* collection)

*The Cattle Point Lighthouse overlooks the site of countless maritime mishaps. Some say a ghostly fighter plane of World War II-vintage haunts the skies above.*
(Bureau of Land Management collection)

*The San Juan County courthouse serves to deter lawbreakers in more ways than one, if the terrifying tales of former jail inmates are to be believed.*
(D.A.H.P. collection)

*The lighthouse at Lime Kiln Point is said to be haunted by a ghostly "sea captain"... perhaps one of the many men to meet their untimely end at the picturesque point.*
(San Juan Island Historical Society collection)

*The University of Washington's Friday Harbor Laboratories, c. 1940s. Once known as Channel Prairie, the land is home to the lost grave of convicted killer Richard Straub.*
(San Juan Island Historical Society collection)

*Few Friday Harbor structures can rival the historic happenings of the Whale Museum. A one-time courthouse, the building bore witness to the island's only hanging in 1897.*
(Chris Light collection)

*The old "haunted cabin" on Cady Mountain as it appeared in the 1970s. The strange tales whispered about the site were never what they seemed . . .* (Journal of the San Juans collection)

*The remote forest around Mt. Grant and Cady Mountain is said to be the home of a rare "subterranean" sasquatch . . .* (Washington State Historical Society collection)

# The Ghost Plane

In a strange echo of the earlier "mysterious aero-planes and airships" seen over Canada during the First World War, a ghostly fighter of World War II-vintage is said to haunt the airspace off Cattle Point—a chilling reminder of the numerous fatal crashes that occurred there during the hectic war years, when the skies over the Sound region were abuzz with all-manner of naval aircraft.

An Argyle resident named Judith Bingham* reported such a sighting in the early 2000s—one that turned an ordinary outing to the Cattle Point Lighthouse into a spine-tingling brush with the unknown. Judith, a frequenter of the area's many trails and scenic overlooks, had parked at the picnic-area pullout on a foggy day and wandered down through the rabbit-warrened dunes to the water's edge, her goldendoodle Lucy in tow. As she passed by the weatherstreaked lighthouse, however, she was confronted by a sight that she would never forget.

"Lucy started acting very oddly," recalls Judith. "She started whining and pulling at her leash [...] I didn't know what was the matter until I saw this plane swoop overhead like a huge bird. I say like a bird because it was completely silent. It was a big airplane, something from the war-era, certainly, and it was painted navy blue with big Air Force or Navy star emblems on the wings. My dad was a P-51 pilot during the war, and I knew it wasn't a P-51, but it reminded me of that. This plane was only about fifty or sixty feet off the ground, and I could see the propeller moving, but it didn't make a sound. Not even of rushing air. I watched it pass over the lighthouse and go out to sea, and it disappeared into this huge fogbank that was covering the water. I had the strangest feeling afterward [...] this eerie, empty kind of feeling, like I'd just witnessed a death or some-thing. It occurred to me that maybe the plane had been gliding, but then there would have been a crash—and I didn't hear a thing."

When Judith returned home, she telephoned the Port of Friday Harbor office at the local airport and reported what she had seen. She was told that the airport had no records of any warbirds in the skies over San Juan at the time of the supposed crash. Nevertheless, she knew what she had seen, and began to dig further into the incident. What she found would leave her deeply shaken.

"I started by trying to identify exactly what kind of plane I had seen," says Judith. After a brief perusal through one of her late father's reference books, she soon found the answer: it was a Grumman F6F Hellcat, a carrier-based fighter used extensively during the Second World War. And, more to the point, a number of such aircraft had been lost in the waters off Cattle Point during training mishaps.

Roughly sixty years before, on November 5th, 1943, a Hellcat piloted by Lieutenant Paul Donhowe had collided with a Canadian P-40 just a few miles south of the point. As the official incident report later stated,

[Donhowe] *was division leader at the time of accident and engaged in division tactics. Several Canadian fighters made runs on the division using an altitude advantage of three or four thousand feet. While the F6F was in a steep, climbing turn, one of the attacking fighters collided with him, the port wing striking just aft of the cockpit. The Canadian fighter did not lose his wing but did spin in after the pilot bailed out. The tail of the F6F slowly twisted off, the pilot bailed out and then plane crashed into water.*

*Could not find the pilot. Wasn't wearing new type chute with life boat attached. He did have on a life jacket, however.*

Neither Lieutenant Donhowe, nor his Hellcat—or

the Royal Canadian Air Force P-40, for that matter—were ever recovered.

Another such tragedy occurred in the same area, on February 1st, 1944. A young ensign named Vernon Spalding was attempting his first-ever carrier landing on the USS *Casablanca* when the arresting cable—meant to slow the aircraft's momentum with the use of a tailhook—gave way and racketed the aircraft left and over the side. The Hellcat plunged thirty feet off the flightdeck and headlong into the spooling currents of the Strait of Juan de Fuca. Ensign Spalding was seen to escape the cockpit, but was soon entangled in the lanyard of his life raft and drowned before a rescue could be mounted.

"I was, and am, pretty much convinced that what I saw was a ghost," says Judith. "I'd welcome a more rational explanation, but that's something I haven't found yet. Lucy started acting very skittish whenever I'd take her on the lighthouse trail, and eventually I just stopped taking her there at all. There's still quite a heavy atmosphere around there, especially on foggy days."

# The Ghost of Cady Mountain

*The* Journal *carried the following story in its Halloween issue of 1978, as written by Anita Melanie Garrett:*

The story of The Ghost of Cady Mountain was told by my late stepfather, Harry Wilks, Sr., and the facts are repeated here substantially as he recounted it. I wish it could be expressed in his exact words, with their hint of Irish brogue, well sprinkled with expletives, but that isn't possible.

One fine moonlit night in about the year 1912 when Harry had newly arrived on San Juan Island, a group of the more exuberant young blades of the north end pooled their resources to buy whiskey for a spree. They carried their booze to a glade on the slope of Cady Mountain where their revels would not disturb the more sedate citizens.

The revelry was scarcely underway when a great black cloud loomed over the shoulder of the mountain, and a clap of thunder rent the air.

"Boys, she's gonna rain!" someone cried, "We're gonna get soaked!"

Another carouser recalled the deserted cabin at the edge of the glade and suggested they seek shelter in it.

"Not me!" came the reply, "That there cabin is haunted!"

The first big drops pelted down and without more ado, they gathered up their whiskey and made a run for the cabin. They pushed open the door, its rusty hinges shrieking like a tortured soul, and a rank musty smell greeted them. The last ones, including a pair who carried a gunny sack containing the whiskey bottles, had barely crowded in when a loud thump sounded on the ceiling. A series of staccato stumps followed, which sounded like the dragging of a ball and chain across the floor.

The revelers burst from the cabin but paused when they reached the trees on the far side of the glade.

"Aw, come on, boys," said some brave soul, "There ain't no such thing as ghosts."

The thunder again rolled out, and in the instantaneous flash of lightning, they saw a horrible apparition in the upper window—a shapeless white form with a long cadaverous face staring out with blazing eyes.

Yelling with terror, they took to their heels and didn't stop until they reached the road at the foot of the mountain. Shuddering, one after another told tales he had heard about the cabin. The last occupant was a mysterious drifter who had disappeared without a trace, leaving all his possessions behind. The one who told the tale had himself seen the frying pan hanging from a nail by the stove, a stalagmite of bacon grease reaching up where it had dripped repeatedly.

Another recalled that a hunter, lost on the mountain on a dark night, had come upon the cabin, its windows all covered, except where chinks of light showed around the edges. He peeked in and saw some men playing cards, each with a gun lying on the table besides great stacks of chips and money. Others recalled tales of violence, murder, strange cries, eerie shapes hovering about, and other ghostly happenings.

"Well, I sure could use a good drink, now that the rain has let up," some one said, "Pass me a bottle."

"Bottle?" came an agonized voice, and the devastating realization came over them that the pair carrying the liquor had left it behind in the cabin.

"I'll give five bucks to anyone who'll go back and get our booze," said one of the thirsty characters.

"Not me!" came a chorus, "I wouldn't go back there for love nor money."

"Okay—I'll make it ten dollars—twenty?"

Now to Harry Wilks, who supported himself with odd jobs, twenty dollars was a lot of money. Besides, he didn't believe in ghosts. Or did he? Something he had heard kept nagging at his mind. What was it? It might be a clue to the mystery—also he surely could use a drink himself, wet to the skin as he was.

"Twenty dollars?" he called out, "I'll take ya up on it."

Some tried to dissuade him, but he took off up the mountain, singing an Irish song.

The clouds passed and the moon shone out, reviving the courage of the revelers. They decided to follow Harry back up the mountain and see what happened.

Cautiously they paused at the edge of the glade. The cabin was silent. There was no sign of Harry.

Then a terrible ruckus broke out in the cabin. First came a pandemonium of thumps, then wild shouts. Suddenly there was a sound of broken glass and rending wood. A huge white form burst out of the window and headed toward them.

To a man, the revelers took off down the mountain as though Satan himself were after them—as they probably thought he was. Again they collected at the roadside.

"Poor Harry!" panted one of his friends. "We'll never see him alive again." The others nodded, and one or two removed their hats.

"Listen!" cried some one, and they heard Harry's voice in the distance, belting out his favorite Irish song:

*Oh, it's old but its beautiful,*

*The best you've ever seen,*
*'Twas wore for more than ninety years,*
*That little isle so green—*
*'Tis the hat me faa-ther wore.*

They stood in stunned silence until Harry appeared, the sack of liquor on his shoulder—and apparently he had sampled the contents before starting down the mountain.

"Any of you guys seen a white goat?" he called.

"Goat? You must mean ghost."

"Naw, I mean goat. That ghost was nuthin' but an old white billy—been in and outa that cabin for a long time, way it looked. I chased him out."

"But—didja know it was a goat when ya went back up there?"

"We-ell—I thought about that smell when we went in—it sure wasn't sulphur and brimstone nor a graveyard, but I couldn't place it right away. Then I recollected that feller kept goats and right away it come to me. Now do I get my twenty bucks?"

And after the Ghost of Cady Mountain had been liberally toasted, he did.

# The Ghost Ship

Much like the fabled "ghost plane" that haunts the fog-shrouded skies over Cattle Point, a fiery, phant-asmic ship has been reported by terrified onlookers for generations—a supposed remnant of the *Transport*, a packet steamer that burned up in a summer storm in 1911.

The *Transport* had been hauling nearly two tho-usand barrels of burned lime from the Roche Harbor kilns when it caught fire off Cattle Point in August of 1911. An unseasonably strong wind had risen abruptly in the night, and now buffeted the one hundred and eleven-foot steamer in the churning strait between Smith Island and San Juan. The danger was not from sinking in the storm, however—it was from the deadly cargo barreled in the hold. Burned lime, when exposed to water, undergoes an exothermic reaction called "slaking," which results in a great deal of fiery heat being generated. Aboard the *Transport*, a small leak had sprung in the hold—and, while it wasn't enough to sink the ship, it was enough to wash the lime with seawater, and to cause the wooden decks to burst into flames.

Though the crew fought hard to save the ship, their efforts were in vain—"Water seemed only to add fuel to the flames," recalled a survivor named Walter Allenby. The lifeboat was lowered, and the men escaped into the pitch-black swells.

"We did not attempt to make shore for fear the lifeboat would swamp, with its heavy load of fifteen men, so we stayed in the light made by the burning vessel in the hope we would be picked up," said Allenby.

Fortunately for the shipwrecked crew, the lights of the guttering inferno were spotted by campers at Burrows Bay, on Fidalgo Island, some fourteen miles distant. A nimble launch was dispatched, and in the end all but one of the crewmen were rescued. An engineer named Wilbur Snyder missed his footing while attempting to cross between the lifeboat and the launch and was "carried away in the heavy seas," according to Allenby. The blazing hulk of the *Transport* finally went down some hours later.

For years afterward, islanders claimed to have sighted the ethereal shade of the doomed ship as it appeared off Cattle Point on certain summer nights—

sometimes heralding a similarly unseasonable storm, according to some. These bone-chilled witnesses typically recalled a strange, fiery light on the black straits, that winked and dipped as though ravaged by an invisible storm, even on calmer nights. Oddly enough, some have described the ship as a masted sailing schooner of a far earlier age—leading some to link the apparition with the *Tolo* tragedy of 1862.

As described in *Shipwrecks of the San Juans*, the *Tolo* had left San Francisco some weeks before, bound for Victoria and Port Ludlow with twelve aboard; thirty-six-year-old Captain Maloney, whose wife and young children lived in the city, First Mate Francis Byrne, Second Mate William Sherlock, Seamen Sullivan, Nelson, and the Andersen brothers, an unnamed Chinese cook, and four passengers. William Carter, a hulking man with a heavy beard and mustache, had been returning home to Ludlow after a visit to his native Maine. W. Ehlers, a Canadian, was in transit to Ludlow as well. He had shipped from San Francisco under the impression that he would meet a friend in Victoria who could secure him work with the Lands and Works Department of British Columbia—and he had spent his last dollar to do so. When the *Tolo* had stopped over Victoria, however, Ehlers was unable to locate his friend; Captain Maloney took pity on the now-destitute man and offered him a free fare to Port Ludlow, where he could find work at the lumber mill. W. Cox was a California farmer who had decided to make a go of the rich agricultural lands now opened for settlement in the Sound region. R.A. Eddy, a San Francisco man, was a theatrical agent for the actress Joey Gougenheim. He was on his way to Port Townsend, and afterwards Australia; no doubt to secure exotic engagements for his illustrious client. Their ballast, notably, was light; and their spars were quite heavy.

At around six a.m. on February 24th, with sunrise not for another hour, the *Tolo* was caught in a squall off Cattle Point. The winds shrieked from the south and buffeted the ship in a heavy chop, though for the most part all seemed to be stable. Captain Maloney, on duty almost all night, had just retired to his cabin, and Peter Nelson was left at the helm. Disaster struck just five minutes after the changeover.

The southerly wind had shifted to the south-west with enough force and abruptness to send the ship crashing sidelong into the waves. As the *Tolo* rolled over, Captain Maloney sprang up the steps from below, half-dressed, and was thrown into the sea; Nelson, meanwhile, scrambled up the hull as she rolled and managed to grab ahold of the keel. All but Cox and Eddy had been thrown overboard. The two were presumed to have drowned in their berths.

Nelson helped First Mate Byrne to safety, and the two immediately began attempting to save the others. Spotting Sullivan clinging to the hull, they thought quickly and tied their jackets together, extending a sleeve of the apparatus to the wayward seaman and hauling him up. From their relative safety atop the overturned hull, the trio could now take in the nightmarish scene.

Second Mate Sherlock, Ehlers, the Andersen brothers, and the Chinese cook were all in the water, and "exerting themselves to the utmost to scale the sides," as Byrne reported. But their efforts were in vain—the survivors could only look on in horror as the men succumbed to the freezing waves, dropping off one by one and sinking to the depths with "despairing cries and looks" until only Captain Maloney was left. Carter, meanwhile, had found a few pieces of debris large enough to keep him afloat, and he called out that he would "try and make the shore." He then struck out towards the darkened coast of San Juan Island.

Captain Maloney is said to have remained perfectly calm despite his dire predicament. He clung to the mainchains, the iron plates fastened to the ship's side that anchored the mainmast rigging, and shouted suggestions over the shrieking wind on how best to assist him. The trio again attempted the method used to rescue Sullivan, and extended their tied-together coats to the captain. They had pulled him up almost all the way before a knot slipped and he fell back into the water. They tried again, this time tying a scarf to an oilskin coat, but the sleeve ripped as soon as Maloney grabbed hold. Several more attempts were made, growing more and more ineffectual as the men grew weaker and numb with cold. Maloney told the men that he could not be saved, but they refused to give up. Eventually, perhaps for the safety of his own men, he looked up and said, "Boys, don't forget my poor wife and children"—and then released his hold on the chains. The captain drifted astern of the *Tolo*, his arms spread out, his head just above the surface of the swells. As Byrne described:

"Occasionally he would raise his head, and gaze wistfully and sadly towards the floating wreck above him, and at the men clinging to it, then his head would slowly droop again. When he had floated about half a length astern he raised his head, as with a last effort, from the water, called out feebly, 'Boys, don't forget my poor wife and children'." He then raised his arms above his head and went down.

Their captain gone, the men now looked about for Carter, and he was soon spotted. Dawn was approaching, and the lone swimmer was visible in the grey light for about ten minutes, making little, if any, progress against the waves. Eventually, he too vanished.

Byrne, Nelson, and Sullivan clung to the keel for fifty-six full hours. They were lashed by wind, snow, and waves that occasionally crashed high and broke over the hull. The squalls carried them northeast, and soon the wreck had drifted close to the shore of Lopez Island, roughly seven miles distant. They had no food, nothing dry, and could only huddle together for warmth and hope that a ship would pass by. In the kind of weather that had capsized their own vessel, however, such a chance would be slim.

But a ship did come. The sloop *Random*, on its way

from Port Townsend to Victoria, hove in sight at around two p.m. on Wednesday the 26th and rescued the men, who by then presented a shocking appearance; being starved, half-dead and badly frostbitten. The *Random* delivered the survivors to Victoria by two a.m. the next morning. All three lived.

A collection was taken up for the men by the citizenry, and soon the Victoria newspapers had extracted the full story from Byrne—undoubtedly an unpleasant experience so soon after the ordeal. Considerable relief was reportedly felt that the Cox who had perished was not John Cox, a well-known Victoria man, as had been falsely stated in earlier news pieces.

The *Tolo* floated about aimlessly for some days afterwards. By Thursday it had drifted into Griffin Bay, and men were placed on the keel to keep an eye on things until a wrecker could arrive. On Saturday it floated out again with the tide, and soon it had returned to Lopez, still trailing the sails, rigging, and spars that had allegedly sealed its doom. The *Random* soon returned, with Byrne aboard, and set about maneuvering the wreck to a safe moorage with a cable and kedge anchor. This completed, the *Tolo*'s creditors received a $12,000 insurance payout, and the matter was considered closed. The schooner itself was towed to Port Townsend by the steam-tug *Resolute* and refurbished; she was again running between Victoria and San Francisco by October of that year.

Notably, witnesses of the supposed "ghost ship" off Cattle Point described a blazing schooner—and

171

while the *Tolo* is the only wreck that fits the bill, there were no flames involved in her demise.

On a more "realistic"—though unsettling—note, a submerged "ghost ship" with a mind of its own was said to have caused a great deal of deluged destruction during the early 1990s. In December of 1991, the derelict one-hundred-and-thirty-nine-foot fishing boat *Ocean Champion* was anchored off the Roche Harbor marina. The listing *Champion* quickly became known as an eyesore and a potential navigation hazard, and concerned islanders noted that it contained some six hundred gallons of diesel fuel. Local pressure mounted, and eventually the Coast Guard and Army Corps of Engineers intervened. The *Champion*, which was found to have shoddy plywood patching and overworked bilge pumps, was drained of its fuel and towed to a site west of Stuart Island. Coast Guardsmen pumped thousands of gallons of seawater into the hulk, and finally it succumbed "with its bow pointing skyward like a prize fighter thrusting his chin high after his final bout," as the *Journal* reported. The *Champion* plunged six hundred feet to the bottom of Haro Strait.

The next year, when the Orcas Power and Light Company's undersea power cable was mysteriously severed, some pointed to the wreck of the *Ocean Champion*.

"The story goes that divers have seen this 140-foot 'ghost ship' cruising our channels at a depth of 90 feet, in an upright position," wrote John Roth in a letter to the *Journal*. Roth theorized that the wooden wreck, as "reluctant to go down as it was," had slowly settled to a depth where the greater pressures had rendered it weightless in the black abyss.

"I see a remote possibility that this cruising hulk may have snagged or bumped our marine cable as it passed Pear Point at an undetermined depth and time," wrote Roth.

The current status of the *Champion* is unknown—if indeed the old troller *has* risen from her watery grave off Turn Point.

Perhaps the oddest of all the accounts is that of the *Clallam* wreckage. According to an old anecdote—of unknown origin, naturally—a San Juan farmer named Johnson stumbled across a welter of detritus washed ashore on the beach below his farm in January of 1904. Days before, the Mosquito Fleet steamer *Clallam* had broken up in a storm just south of San Juan, taking fifty-six souls to a watery grave in what would prove to be one of the worst maritime disasters in Puget Sound history. Now, Johnson had found the terrifying remnants of the tragedy—pieces of splintered wood, clothing, personal effects, and random fittings, all apparently deposited by a fateful current. The piece that Johnson kept was a finely-figured lounge chair from the galley or smoking-room—it was in good enough condition that Johnson presented it to his wife, claiming that he had purchased it from the Sears catalog.

Johnson's wife refused to sit in the chair, however;

it reeked of saltwater and was always cold, despite its placement by the woodstove. Still, Johnson kept the chair. It was the finest piece of furniture they owned, and it was a gift, after all. But his tune would finally change when he and his wife returned from town one evening to find their little cabin shaking and splitting apart as though caught in a violent earthquake! Despite the ground remaining perfectly still, the chinking was crumbling and the logs beginning to dislodge as the cedarshakes sloughed from the roof like maple leaves in a fall wind; and somehow, Johnson knew precisely what the cause was. He ran inside the spasming cabin, which to Johnson now seemed more like the deathly, disintegrating throes of a ship as she breaks apart on the final plunge to the bottom, and grabbed the accursed chair. He sprinted to the shore and heaved it into the outgoing tide—and, upon returning, found the cabin to be still again, and largely whole. The real thrashing would come later, no doubt, when he confessed the truth to his wife.

# The Haunted Lighthouse

The picturesque lighthouse at Lime Kiln Point, above the ominous Dead Man's Bay, has guided ships through Haro Strait for well over one hundred years. The Light presents a timeless portrait of the classical American lighthouse; a whitewashed facade, sea-green trim, and a red-tiled roof, situated on a jagged point extending out from the groves of ancient madrona and wind-twisted fir. And although now a popular wedding venue and a haven for hikers and whale-watchers, the land has a rather dark history only hinted at by the bay's terrifying toponym.

Just who the Dead Man was, no one can now say. According to legend, the name derived from the bodies of trafficked Chinese laborers that often washed ashore there in the late 19th century. Smugglers like Ben Ure and "Pirate" Larry Kelly were notorious for their supposed practice of binding up their human cargo in potato sacks and heaving them overboard when the threat of arrest made such an action convenient. With no "Celestials" aboard, the smugglers could pass as simple fishermen. Another, more plausible explanation was offered by Edmond S. Meany, a noted student of San Juan Islands etymology. As Meany wrote in his 1923 *Origin of Washington Geographic Names*, "It is claimed that the first white man known to have died on the island was buried there. He was a working man killed by a cook." Though Meany does not identify the specific case, it can be inferred that this was likely the Wheeler murder, which took place at the Lyman Cutlar homestead in 1863 (see the "American Camp" chapter of this book). Other versions stated that the victim had been thrown into the strait and had washed up at the bay, or that he had been killed at the site. Etta Egeland, however, the founder of the San Juan Island Historical Society, claimed that "an unnamed white man criticized a Chinese cook at the Lime Kiln, who killed him with a knife. The Chinese was aided to escape from San Juan Island by a farmer named Bailer, who hid him in a wagon until he found a vessel that was leaving from Friday Harbor." The veracity of this account remains unknown—although considering that the name "Dead Man" appeared on nautical charts as far back as the early 1860s, Meany's theory is likely the correct one.

Regardless of the Dead Man's identity, the land surrounding the old lighthouse has a long and colorful history. It first attracted attention in the 1860s, when settlers had noted the sheer cliffs of pale limestone rearing up along the western shore near the present-day Light. Lyman Cutlar, E.C. Gillette, and David F. Newsom staked a claim near Dead Man's Bay in 1860, about a month prior to the arrival of British troops, and burned lime in a crude kiln there until 1864, when the three partners sold out their interest to a man named Augustin Hibbard. Hibbard was one of the shady characters so often scorned by the island's military commanders—a typical scofflaw who made his living smuggling and selling cheap liquor to soldiers and Indians alike. By 1869, he was running the limeworks with a new set of partners, among them a man named Charles Watts—and on June 17th of that year, a series of disputes between the two men would come to a horrifying head.

That evening, the two confronted each other at the company office, which was then located in the old boarding house. The two quarreled over an Indian woman "kept by Hibbard," and over several items which Hibbard accused Watts of stealing. As the *Washington Standard* reported, "Words ran high, and Watts drawing a revolver, presented it close to Hibbard's face, firing three shots, all of which took effect; one in the forehead, another under the right eye, and the third in the lower part of the left cheek. Hibbard, strange to say, after this walked down stairs;

on reaching the room below he exclaimed, 'It's of no use, I am a dead man,' and fell dead upon the floor."

Watts was detained by the kiln workers and presented to the American Camp commander. Because the murder had taken place in the disputed San Juans, his court proceedings lasted for seven years, through numerous trials and appeals, until it eventually reached the Territorial Supreme Court in Olympia. The justices upheld Watts's guilty verdict, and the murderer was sentenced to hang in 1876. In April of that year, however, he escaped from the Kitsap County Jail. As was later reported, "He and two other convicts were being marched back to the jail, when, taking advantage of the turned back of the guard, Watts struck out for freedom. It was nearly dark, the brush was close by, and in a moment he was out of sight." Charles Watts was never seen again.

The kilns were eventually deeded to James McCurdy, of Port Townsend, to cover Hibbard's outstanding debts. Shortly after, McCurdy himself went into debt and was forced to lease the diggings to John S. McMillin in 1886. Only a month after the transaction, however, McCurdy sold the site to McMillin's arch-rival, Henry Cowell. Cowell made a rather ingenious play to buy it out from under McMillin—he ceased mortgage payments, forcing McMillin to foreclose, and then purchased the property at the bankruptcy auction. It was another move in the decades-long chess match between the magnates, and for years afterward the place was known as Cowell's.

The Lime Kiln Light was first established in 1914. A rudimentary acetylene beacon and foghorn were constructed on the point, as the Lighthouse Board had recognized the need for such a signal as far back as 1908. After only a few years, however, it had become apparent that a proper lighthouse would be required, with the commission noting that:

"Vessels proceeding to the northward after leaving Point Wilson have a run of about 32 miles before reaching the proposed location, with no fog signal on the American side. The depths are too great for soundings and there are strong tidal currents of uncertain direction to contend with. A light and fog-signal station will provide a definite point to run for in going north through Haro Strait, and a definite point of departure for vessels bound across the treacherous eastern end of Juan de Fuca Strait for Puget Sound, or bound northward through Haro Strait. This location is where it is customary for vessels to change course. It is important to the mariner that he verify his position here or in this vicinity in order to avoid the dangers on both sides of this narrow strait."

Construction on the Light complex commenced in August of 1918. The tower was built of reinforced concrete about twenty feet above the high-tide mark, with a fourth-order Fresnel lens installed in a seven-foot helical-bar lantern room that revolved the cut gem of the light over a mercury float and shone the haunting beam over the moonlit strait. On the hillside above, a handsome pair of bungalows were built to house the keepers. All in all, the Lime Kiln Point station shaped up to become one of the more desirable postings in the Lighthouse Service retinue. Officially opened on June 30th, 1919, it was the last major lighthouse constructed in the state of Washington.

It was also the last lighthouse in the state to be electrified—up until 1951, the Light had relied on a system of kerosene vapor piped up to the incandescent lamp with compressed air. With a submarine power cable finally running to the islands, the aged Fresnel lens was replaced with a static three hundred and seventy-five-millimeter drum lens with an electric light bulb. The Light was administered by the Coast Guard, and by 1962 was fully automated. Today, it is still in regular service as both a beacon and a whale-watching center, and the surrounding lands are a state park.

With such a storied history, it is little wonder that spooky tales have often been told about the old Lime Kiln Light. Stories have long circulated of the ubiquitous phantom footsteps and brief whiffs of an unseen smoker's pipe tobacco. One such yarn is told by marine mammal biologist David Bong, who spent a number of months at Lime Kiln Point as a researcher and docent—the Friday Harbor-based Whale Museum having leased the lighthouse as an interpretive center since 1984.

"It is a great location, probably one of the best," says Bong. "The bottom drops off to nine hundred and something feet just a few yards offshore, and you'll get orcas, greys, Minkes, porpoises, all kinds of incredible cetaceans. Part of my job was to help run the hydrophone, which is a remote sensor for picking up whale vocalizations and other sounds that's set up in the lighthouse. It's really an incredible system. So I spent a lot of time in the lighthouse.

"One day, I was alone in the lighthouse and it was a very stormy day. We got some pretty big storms off the strait sometimes [...] the winds could get up to sixty miles an hour, which can make the place pretty spooky with the drafts swirling around in the tower and making this moaning kind of sound. My kind-of supervisor Darcy* left about a half hour before, and I was about to close up [...] it was getting late in the afternoon, and with all this wind, I was just hoping to get home before a tree fell and blocked the road. So, as I'm locking up outside, I started to feel like someone was watching me. You know that feeling when the hairs on the back of your neck start to stand up? It was that. I looked around and I didn't see anyone, though, so I started walking up to the parking lot [...] but something told me to turn around. Or not to turn around. I'm not sure which [...] either way, I knew that if I turned around, I would see whoever or whatever was watching me. And when I did, there was a person standing inside the glass of the beacon room. To me, it looked like an old sea captain. He had a grey beard and a captain's hat, and like a peacoat or a long coat with brass buttons. And he was staring right at me—and then he was just gone. In the blink of an eye. Like he was never there."

In what seems to be a common theme for supernatural sightings on San Juan Island, Bong ran all the way back to his car. Naturally, the lighthouse had been empty, and no one was to be found there the next morning.

"I never liked working in there after that, and, in all honesty, that was one of the main reasons why I decided to move on from volunteering there," says Bong.

What ghost might haunt the old Lime Kiln Light? That of a lighthouse keeper, perhaps, or a captain of one the countless ships that met their doom in the wild strait? Or could it be a shade from the old kilns—Augustin Hibbard or Thomas Wheeler, whose lonely grave lies somewhere near the windswept point? The answer, as usual, might only be found with a visit to the spectacular vistas of Lime Kiln Point— to watch for whales, or for other things . . .

# *Big Bones*

Though far more prevalent on the neighboring isles of Orcas, Lummi, and Cypress, the legendary sasquatch, or bigfoot, is indeed alleged to roam the remote hills and valleys of San Juan Island. Since the earliest days of human habitation, stories have circulated of monstrous giants whom the Lummi called *Ts'emekwes*, or "Big Bones," a race of eight-foot-tall, nocturnal creatures that stalked hunters, stole salmon from reefnets, and, occasionally, snatched naughty children from unguarded longhouses—habits, it would seem, that have somewhat endured into the present day.

Contrary to the many dark-haired depictions of sasquatch, Big Bones was known for its light coat and white face; attributes that allowed it to blend seamlessly into snowy surroundings.

"There are many traditions concerning [Big

Bones] told within the Lummi community," writes historian Stacy Rasmus. "In fact, most community members are able to recall a telling concerning this particular figure."

These giants, apparently a subspecies akin to the white-haired spirit bears of coastal British Columbia, were said to inhabit the many lime-stone caves that honeycomb the islands. Mostly dormant during daylight hours, they would emerge from their stony warrens at odd hours of the night to wander the forests undetected. Their fearsome appearance, as described in tribal lore, has led some to categorize the San Juan Sasquatch as an arcane and nightmarish remnant of the long-vanished *Gigantopithecus*, though such theories are generally dismissed out of hand by the more scientifically-minded. Other accounts of Big Bones depict a more human-like creature—a tribe of "lost humans," perhaps, more neolithic than primeval. Still, regardless of its taxonomy, *Ts'emekwes* was known to be dangerous—and hungry.

Big Bones is still reported with semi-regularity even outside the present-day Lummi Nation, where strange sightings are a part of everyday life. 1975 was a standout year for such activity; on the reservation, which overlooks the San Juans, a rash of more than one hundred reports was recorded, including several from a tribal police sergeant.

"Sgt. [Ken] Cooper said so many people were chasing the Sasquatch with guns that the Lummi tribal council voted to outlaw shooting the creature," stated the *Vancouver Sun* in November of that year.

This wave of sightings seemingly spilled over into the former Lummi lands, as well. On San Juan Island, in December of 1975, a hunter named Leonard Spear had a run-in with the hirsute biped that left him shaken for days. As Spear told it, he had gone out to bag a blacktail on what is now the Mount Grant Preserve, a large and undeveloped tract of old-growth timber above Trout Lake, when the unimaginable occurred.

As Spear stalked alongside the narrow creek that burbles down from Newt Pond, he spotted what he initially believed to be an old stump sitting by the bank. As he neared, however, the "stump" shifted on its heels—it was, in fact, a hairy humanoid squatting by the stream and scooping up water with its man-like hands!

Though armed with a deer rifle, Spear reported that he felt little fear in the creature's presence. "It didn't seem threatening," he later told his daughter. Spear watched as the Big Bones stood, perhaps catching his scent, and strode away into the trees, apparently "not the least bit bothered."

A more terrifying account comes from former islander Steve Minnett. In the early 1980s, Minnett had moved from California and secured a job at a small rock quarry near Sportsman's Lake. He found lodging in a "funky" old trailer about a mile away, on a large and remote property below Cady Mountain.

"The rent was dirt cheap, but [the place] always

felt off," recalls Minnett. "It got to where I'd try to spend as little time there as I could. I just used the place for sleeping most of the time. But even then, I'd wake up and hear all kinds of stuff out in the woods."

Minnett's encounter came on a grey morning in February of 1982. His alarm clock sounded at seven, and he rose and trimmed his beard and fried a pair of eggs on the Coleman range. As he stepped outside, half-asleep, the sun still hadn't risen above the tall trees—and off in the murky woods, several yards away, something stirred.

"I heard sticks breaking and something big rustling in the bushes," says Minnett. Though at first believing he had startled a deer, the groggy quarryman was quickly corrected when a massive, upright-walking creature emerged from the dark treeline. About eight feet tall and covered in shaggy fur, the biped loped out of woods and cut across the edge of the small clearing, giving Minnett a sufficient look at the unexpected visitor.

"It was carrying a dead deer," recalls Minnett, seeming to shudder at the memory. "Blood all over the place, neck broken. It was a big buck, and this thing was carrying it like a stuffed animal. Like it weighed nothing."

Minnett watched in frozen horror as the sasquatch entered the woods again and climbed up the mountainside behind the trailer.

"All of a sudden, all the weird feelings and weird sounds I'd been hearing made sense," he reflects.

Having long since returned to California, he adds curtly: "I haven't felt the need to go back."

The quarryman's tale is echoed by longtime islander Grace Brainerd*, whose similarly isolated home sits on the southern slopes of Cady Mountain about two miles from Minnett's trailer. Brainerd, an artist, often finds inspiration in nature, and would frequently wander the small trails crisscrossing the extensive property while her husband Larry* worked at his Friday Harbor office. One area in particular proved especially meditative—a limestone outcropping, far from the house, that concealed a mossy, fern-draped grotto.

"It looked like a little cave," wrote Grace in correspondence with the author, "but it only went back a few feet. It reminded me of a grotto like you'd see in an old English or Japanese garden, so I put a little pagoda inside the entrance. I'd go there all the time."

One morning—around the same time of day as Minnett's sighting, it would seem—Grace went out to the grotto to practice her daily transcendental meditation. To her surprise, however, she found that the small cement pagoda had been knocked over.

"I suppose an animal could have done it, but for some reason I just knew it *wasn't* an animal," says Grace. Moments later, her suspicions were confirmed when Big Bones itself appeared out of the trees.

"It was a sasquatch, certainly, but it was a very young one. It had almost blonde fur, like how some

187

babies are born blonde but their hair turns dark with age. This magnificent creature walked easily towards me and stopped at the grotto entrance. It had the most wonderfully kind eyes I have ever seen. It stopped and very deliberately picked up the pagoda and set back the way it had been. And it gave me a glance, with such a wise expression that I experienced this kind of euphoria, this weightlessness that I had been trying to reach through my meditation. It climbed into the grotto and moved aside this boulder at the back that had been blocking the rest of the tunnel. I felt a cool wind rush out the cave, and the scent of earth and wildflowers. The young sasquatch gave me one final look and disappeared into the cave, and its hands reached out and pulled the boulder back into place. With that it was gone, and I never saw my young sasquatch friend again."

Rumors of an extensive cave system in the limestone beneath Cady Mountain lend a degree of credence to Grace's tale—though the system's potentially antediluvian inhabitants are another matter. Does the *Ts'emekwes* of Lummi lore skulk through subterranean passages below San Juan Island and emerge from Grace Brainerd's grotto to spread feelings of joy and spiritual peace? Does it drink peacefully from forest streams at the Mount Grant Preserve? Or is it something far more savage, a monstrous, carnivorous giant as reported by Steve Minnett? Perhaps, as with all things, only time will tell.

# A Hanging at the Whale Museum

"VILLAINOUS MURDER" blared the local newspaper. Alongside lurid headlines telling of Dr. H.H. Holmes and his Chicago "Murder Castle," the *Islander* of September 5th, 1895 reported that a forty-nine-year-old schoolteacher named Richard Straub had committed a similarly savage atrocity much closer to home. He and a teenaged accomplice named Parberry had ambushed the teacher's rivals at a Blakely Island farmstead and opened fire on the unarmed harvesters, killing one and wounding another. It was "the most atrocious, brutal and cowardly murder ever chronicled in this section of the state," declared the editor, and the killer would hang for it. It would be the first, and last, public execution ever carried out in San Juan County, and it occurred in Friday Harbor.

The tall, red-haired Straub had moved to Blakely in 1889, when he purchased the former homestead of ex-lime kiln man E.C. Gillette on the southwestern end of the island. All was not immediately well, however—as historian David Richardson related,

"Actually, Straub had preferred a piece of land adjoining Gillette's, and tried to homestead it; but was beat out of it—as he reckoned—by one J.C. Burns, a railroad man who wasn't even home most of the time. Burns' place was run by his wife, Pauline, daughter of the pioneer Lanterman family of Decatur Island."

On an island as isolated and tight-knit as Blakely, especially in the early days, it was usually best to keep a lid on such disputes; after all, men carried firearms, and arguments could sometimes descend into madness. Straub managed to put his differences aside enough to secure a position as teacher at the little log school—Pauline Burns being the school board clerk. "But bad blood between Straub and the Lanterman clan (though Straub always professed to get along well with the absent Burns) marred the set-up," wrote Richardson. Straub, incidentally, had been a teacher in Coupeville in the early 1880s—but had been forced out after a failed lawsuit over the minutiae of his contract.

Sentiments on Blakely were beginning to turn against the schoolteacher, furthered more so by Straub's widely-publicized brush with the law in May of 1893. On the 10th of that month, the steamship *J.C. Brittain* had gone aground on Belle Rock in a heavy fog four miles south of Blakely. It had been a dramatic scene; as a passenger described,

> *When we entered the fog the mate gave the slow bell, but there was a strong tide which ran like a mill race, and we had only been in the fog a few minutes when we struck the rocks, at 5:15 a.m., just after daylight. The boat struck amidship. Orders were at once given to back, but she was fast with a hole in her bottom, through which water came into the hold. She listed badly to port and filled rapidly, the lime taking fire. The crew and the captain were in their bunks at the time and were immediately aroused. The lifeboat was gotten out and it was not over ten minutes until we left the steamer, but the barrels of lime were already bursting and popping like big firecrackers. Great volumes of steam poured out of her as soon as the water entered, and before we got any distance away the flames shot up.*
>
> *[...] Just after the* Brittain *struck, hundreds of rats came out of the hold and ran upon the bow, which was the highest out of the water. Nothing was saved.*

The charred hulk perched prominently in the strait soon attracted attention. Acting on rumors that the wreck was being stripped bare by illicit salvagemen, the first mate and an insurance adjuster motored out to the reef in a steam launch to investigate. As related in *Shipwrecks of the San Juans*, the pair spotted another boat heading in the same direction, which then abruptly changed course and made for Blakely Island. Suspicious, the mate and the insurance man overtook the boat to question its lone occupant: it was Richard

Straub. In Straub's boat was a demijohn that the mate recognized as having come from the *Brittain*. Suspecting that Straub was hiding a stash of ill-gotten goods, the pair let him continue on, but then beat a course for Straub's homestead. They arrived much quicker in their steam launch and awaited the suspected looter. When Straub finally returned, they asked to look around the place; Straub asked if they had a search warrant. The two replied that they didn't, and Straub produced a Winchester rifle, declaring that if the men didn't clear out he would "put a hole" in them. The first mate and the insurance man complied. Later that day, when they finally inspected the *Brittain*, around two hundred dol-lars-worth of equipment was found to have been purloined.

Straub's wife, Jane, passed away of Bright's disease in May of 1895, around the same time as a school board election which caused a great deal of strife for the little island community. The negative feeling toward Straub had finally come to a head, and now Pauline Burns was openly calling for Straub's dismissal. It was decided that a vote would be held to elect a new teacher—a grim prospect for Straub, as Burns's brother, twenty-three-year-old Leon Lanterman, also sat on the school board. The directors voted two-to-one to replace Straub—Lanterman, of course, being among the majority.

"You godd—n son of a b—h, come outside and we will settle this!" shouted Straub. The two were on the verge of grappling before being restrained.

This school board controversy, combined with the sudden death of his wife, sent the "erstwhile pedagogue" into a spiral of depression and irascibility—a state that only worsened as the summer wore on. In the months leading up to the final incident, Straub claimed that the Lantermans had set fire to a slashpile on the Burns place, which had then spread over to a property belonging to Irving Parberry's brother and destroyed the man's cabin. This was repudiated by the Lanterman faction, who accused Straub himself of setting the fire. Regardless, "the cabin fire seems to have been merely the spark that exploded the bomb," as the newspapers waxed. The fire had followed accusations of Straub slaughtering a pair of cows belonging to the Burnses and various other land disputes. No matter who said what, however, it would all culminate on a late summer evening in August of 1895.

Between five and six o'clock, on the evening of the 30th, Lanterman and his sister were harvesting potatoes at the Burns place. Their step-brother, Ralph Blythe, had also rowed over from Decatur to help. As the *Islander* reported:

[...] *a young fellow named Irving Parberry emerged from the bushes just outside the field, and at once commenced abusing Mr. Lanterman in a scurrilous manner, calling him all sorts of vile and obscene names. Mr. Lanterman soon laid aside his hoe and walked toward young Parberry, asking as he did so, why he talked in that manner to him. Before he got to him Straub arose from behind a log, and both he and Parberry commenced firing at him (Lanterman), Straub with a Winchester rifle and Parberry with a pistol. Two shots took effect, one ball passing through the bowels and one through the arm. Lanterman then turned back and ran, exclaiming to his sister, "I am shot—I am killed." The step-brother, Blythe, went to aid him, and he too was fired upon, but falling upon the ground as if shot he subsequently made his escape.*

*Straub then turned upon Mrs. Burns, using the most obscene language man could utter and saying "Now I will kill you," and began firing at her. She turned to run and his first bullet passed through her right shoulder inflicting a flesh wound near the neck. She continued her flight, running in a zigzag course, and by her doing so escaped being by any one of the several bullets which Straub continued to fire at her as long as there were any left in the magazine of the gun. She reached her house on the beach without further injury and taking a skiff, she and her son Percie, 10 years of age, made their way to Mr. Spencer's and reported the murder as she supposed of both of her brothers. As soon as possible the neighbors were collected and went in a body in search of the missing. Mr. Blythe soon came in unhurt, but Mr. Lanterman's body was found just over the fence, where he lay with one additional bullet through his head, Straub having shot the poor unfortunate man after life was extinct.*

Straub's accomplice was seventeen-year-old Irving Sylvester Parberry, whose family had moved from Amador County, California and homesteaded near Horseshoe Lake in earlier years. Young Parberry gave the following account at the October trial, when he turned state's evidence against his former teacher:

"Straub gave me a six-shooter and ordered me to go with him to the field where the Burnses and Lantermans were at work. At first I refused; but he drew a bead on me, and told me I would have to call and holloa for Leone [sic] Lanterman. Then I went and called to the men in the field. I called to Leone [sic] Lanterman. He was humpbacked, and I holloaed to him: 'You — humpbacked — of a —.' Then, Leone started toward me, and I was standing on a fallen tree, and when he came up to where I was he said: 'What's eating you?' and struck at me. I dodged him and struck him in the back with an ax. Then Lanterman reached for a stick, and as he picked it up off the ground Straub stepped out from behind an upturned stump and yelled: 'You humpbacked — of a —, I have you where I want you now. I'll make you eat hell.'

"When he said that, he shot. Leone Lanterman gave a groan and started back for the field. Just as Straub fired, Ralph Blythe rushed forward with a hoe in his hand, and Blythe pretended to be wounded and dropped; but as Straub came up to where he was and started to fire again, Blythe jumped up and started and ran zigzag, dropping every now and then and darting about. Then Straub saw that Blythe had got away, and so he started up the trail that Leone Lanterman had taken. He told me to follow him, and made me fire the revolver which he gave me. I shot, but as soon as

I saw that Straub was out of sight in the alder bushes along the trail I started and ran to the beach, going toward Straub's house. When I got to his house I broke down the door, got a shotgun and loaded it, and a .32-caliber rifle. Then I went out and hid on the hill, for I was afraid that Straub was going to kill me. He came back in the direction where I had shot, and called me. I could see him, but I did now answer. Then he put his gun down carefully behind a tree and called up toward the house for me. When he got no answer he started toward the house. But he had a dog with him, and the dog got on my trail. When the dog barked Straub looked up the hill and saw me, and he saw, too, that I had him covered with my gun. Then he talked to me for a while, and we went up to the house. He got some more ammunition, and we started for my house. On the way Straub said: 'The hump-backed — of a —. He's as dead as a toad in that potato field. He has always claimed that he lived on Blakely and Decatur Islands, but people won't have to ask where he lives now'."

Parberry, who had worked on Straub's ranch, claimed that "All that I have done was in fear of Straub," and that the schoolteacher had "drilled" him on the story that they would tell authorities—namely, that Lanterman and company had attacked first.

"Straub claims that Lanterman and Blythe began the trouble," reported the *Anacortes American*, "and that Lanterman knocked Parberry down with a club and fired at him before Straub shot. Straub claims to have fired at Lanterman to save Parberry's life. He says that he was passing in a boat when he heard Lanterman abusing Parberry, and thinking there might be trouble, went ashore and climbed the bank just in time to see Parberry knocked down and shot at. He denies shooting at Mrs. Burns or Blythe, but admits having had trouble with Lanterman, but says he never had trouble with Burns or his wife."

Their story straight, the pair set out to turn themselves in. They rowed through the night and arrived in Friday Harbor at around one o'clock that morning. Sheriff Newton Jones, no doubt in shock, locked the murderers away in the little county jail. The news of the horror spread quickly, along with a number of lurid rumors—including that Pauline Burns had spoken to Mrs. Straub on her deathbed, and that the dying woman had accused her own husband of poisoning her.

"This is alleged as a reason why Straub wanted to kill Mrs. Burns," reported the papers. "The story having been made public and Straub's general hard name caused the people to try to do away with his life."

At the same time, Reverend Isaac Dillon delivered a rather inflammatory eulogy at Lanterman's Lopez Island funeral, in what many regarded as more of a "call to arms" than a memorial service. The locals, thoroughly outraged and fired up by the reverend's sermon, grabbed their rifles and set out for San Juan.

Around fifty armed islanders from Blakely, Decatur, and Lopez had gathered at the jail with rope in hand, and Sheriff Jones realized quickly that he and his handful of deputies would be unable to stave off the mob if they decided to storm the hoosegow. Besieged, Jones sent a courier to alert the commander of the local Revenue Cutter that he and his nimble launch would be needed to extradite the prisoners to safety.

"[Straub and Parberry] were taken from the jail about six o'clock, when most of the mob were at supper, and hurried to a mill on the waterfront," reported the *Seattle Post-Intelligencer*.

*They were separately manacled and left in charge of one deputy, while another remained at the jail, apparently still on guard. This action was seen, however, by a picket of the mob stationed on a hill between the jail and water, and he fired his pistol as a signal to the others, who hurriedly gathered in the street. The launch had not arrived, and the sheriff, to gain time, ran in an opposite direction, as if in pursuit of some one, and told the mob one of the prisoners had escaped. The launch steamed past the wharf to the mill, and the sheriff ran to the rendezvous and hurried the prisoners aboard. The mob, nearly all armed with rifles, followed.*

*Lieut. Carden* [Godfrey L. Carden, the launch commander] *drew a pistol, and said he would fire upon any man who fired upon the United States flag, or any man under its protection. His action was taken only after the receipt of a written appeal from the sheriff, setting forth the circumstances and stating that he had no possible way to convey the prisoners to a place of safety.*

In the end, Straub and Parberry were safely carried across to the Whatcom County Jail, where they remained until their trial in October. On the 3rd, Sheriff Jones and a deputy brought the pair back to Friday Harbor, and on the 5th the trial began. The proceedings, the largest of their kind ever held in Friday Harbor, were conducted in the Odd Fellows Hall—the courthouse was too small.

Already condemned in the eyes of the public, Straub didn't have a ghost of a chance. He attempted to hire the famed attorney—and future U.S. senator—J. Hamilton Lewis, but Lewis's conditions were not palatable to Straub, and so he retained a local lawyer named Nordyke and a Seattle counsel named Charles Repath, though he had seriously considered representing himself. Up against the bullet-maimed young mother and her stepbrother, and with Parberry now acting as the state's primary witness, Straub could have hired Clarence Darrow for that all it mattered—the outcome would still be the same. It was in Leon Lanterman's last words, as the *Intelligencer* reported: *Hang Straub.*

Straub did himself no favors during the trial. He stumbled through a long and convoluted recounting on the events which became muddled and confused during cross-examination. It was shortly after mindight on October 20th when the jury reached their widely-predicted verdict of murder in the first degree. The process had dragged on for hours, it was said, because two of the jurors had been firm opponents of the death penalty. But, after a great deal of convincing—and, perhaps, the lateness of the hour—the death penalty was decided upon nonetheless. The *Islander* described the scene:

*The judge and attorneys were notified, and in a few moments the armed guards with Straub handcuffed filed into the dimly lighted hall. The prisoner dropped into a chair, his shoulders drooped, head bowed and brow knitted. His attorneys seated beside whispering into his ears, but he heeded them not, and when the few words were read that sealed his doom, he seemed not to hear it. The solemn midnight hour, the dark and gloomy room—for the hall was dimly lighted—the two rifles and revolver, the blood stained clothing and great hob nailed shoes, the grim and silent witnesses of the bloody drama, lent a weird and ghostly appearance to the scene that impressed one as in keeping with the dark and terrible character of the man who had just been tried.*

As for Parberry, his youth and "weakness" were taken into account, and he was not prosecuted further—"It is to be hoped that the terrible lesson may not be lost upon him and that in the future he may pay more heed to his good mother's counsel, shun evil associates, stop using profane and vulgar language and do his best to merit confidence and trust," said the *Islander*. Perhaps he did; eight years later, Parberry, then described as a "popular young man," married a young woman named Susie Hobart and settled down in Bellingham. They had six children, and Irving Parberry passed away there in 1948.

Straub suffered a severe heart attack in the Whatcom jail, where he was confined pending his final judgment—the physician thought he might die, but he pulled through. In light of his background as an educator, he also served as the magistrate of a "kangaroo court," a kind of mock-tribunal among the prisoners to handle in-house disputes. Meanwhile, a prominent witness in the case, Joseph Prettyman, was arrested in Skagit County—he and an unidentified youth had held up a man for money, but the robbery had gone wrong, and the cohort had fatally stabbed the man as Prettyman held him down. It was an odd turn of events, considering Prettyman had been a school director alongside Lanterman.

On February 18th, 1897, Straub was finally handed down his death date: March 26th. He was calm, reportedly, and seemed to expect that something yet would turn up to "save his neck from the gallows." This would not be the case, though he did receive a one-month respite from the governor, in order to allow the State Board of Pardons "further time in which to examine into the prayer of certain petitioners that the sentence of death upon Mr. Straub be changed to imprisonment for life." The execution day was now set for April 23rd.

The horror of the Kanaka Joe hanging twenty-three years before was still fresh in the minds of all those who had witnessed it, and Sheriff Jones determined that such a thing would not happen again. He erected the gallows on the east side of the jail, on the southeast corner of First and Spring Street, and enclosed the scaffold in a sixteen-foot fence. This time there would be no throngs to ogle the man's final moments; just twenty officials, reporters, and those lucky enough receive a ticket from the sheriff. Jones held off on dropping the trap until a particular steamship arrived which might have borne the news of a last-minute clemency. When the ship failed to bring such news, Sheriff Jones led Straub onto the scaffold and bound up the condemned man's hands and legs and then asked if he had anything he would like to say.

"With a voice almost strangely calm and peaceful he spoke for nearly ten minutes, saying that if nothing but the truth had been spoken at the trial he would never have been condemned to hang," reported the *Intelligencer* correspondent.

*"Nevertheless," he continued, "the trial is past, and I can honestly say that I feel no malice or revenge toward anybody."*

*He talked of religion, and said that since his conversion he had felt better than in all his life before. He thanked the people of Whatcom for their kindnesses during his incarceration there, and likewise the people of Friday Harbor. He expressed gratitude to the Salvation Army, and especially to the woman Salvationist who was present, saying that had it not been for her he would have taken his life weeks ago. Last of all, he thanked Sheriff Jones and bade him good-bye. Not until the very last words did the voice falter even in the slightest degree.*

*Sheriff Jones replied: "Good-bye, Mr. Straub; God bless you."*

Reverend Thomas L. Dyer, the Methodist minister, spoke a few words, and then Sheriff Jones drew the black hood over Straub's head. He felt under Straub's jaw to ensure that the noose was secured properly—recalling Kanaka Joe, no doubt—and then he stepped backward and gave the signal to drop the trap, and Richard Straub plunged down through the hatchway and swung in the morning air, dead, his neck broken instantly.

The county officials oversaw the man's burial in a lone plot on Channel Prairie, a sunny meadow on the military reserve below Point Caution. In years past, the broad grassland had extended up from the harbor's edge to the summit of Sheep Hill—the Hudson's Bay Company had once grazed its flocks there during the autumn months, under the watchful eye of the Hawaiian Joe Friday. Prior to the "Moon of the Snow-Faced Men," the Indians had set controlled fires in the area to allow the cultivation of camas and chocolate lily. With their departure, and the advent of grazing, the forest began to gradually encroach on the borders of the prairie. Saplings of fir and shore pine sprouted up through the fields of bracken and soon overtook the grave of Richard Straub. Today, the site is home to the Friday Harbor Laboratories—and Straub's resting place is lost in the trees.

Today, some contend that the site of the fateful trial still reverberates with echoes of the past. The old Odd Fellows Hall, now the Whale Museum, was built as the Mount Dallas Lodge No. 95 by local members of the International Order of Odd Fellows in 1892. The I.O.O.F. had been a popular fraternity in the San Juans, with a similar lodge built on Orcas the year previous and a membership that spanned the social strata of the islands; such places held high status in their communities. Dances, rallies, religious gatherings, plays, graduations, and all other manner of social events were held in the spacious hall—including the Straub trial, of course. The prominence of the Mount Dallas Lodge only faded in the years following World War II, when returning veterans shunned the I.O.O.F. in favor of the American Legion and other organizations. The lodge had disbanded by the 1950s, and the ceremonial accouterments were donated to the Mount Constitution Lodge in Eastsound—which burned to the ground in 1950.

Faced with potential demolition, the disused hall was finally saved by local arts patron Lee Bave in 1959. Bave, who owned the Mar Vista Resort with her husband Milt, spent a great deal of time and money restoring the aged hall, which was eventually renamed the Island Gallery. The main hall was reopened for community dances and theatrical productions, while the second story—previously the ceremonial chambers of the Odd Fellows—was used for arts-and-crafts classes and similar courses. The Gallery was also home to Bave's long-running production of the *San Juan Saga*, a play outlining the history of the Pig War and other local events.

In 1979, the Baves were visited by noted cetologist and San Juan Island resident Ken Balcomb, who had become interested in establishing a permanent exhibit to educate the public on the importance of orcas and other whales. Balcomb proposed renting the second floor of the Gallery for his "whale museum"—and though Bave was at first skeptical, she later wrote, "I am sure now everyone is proud of their accomplishments and being known thro'out the world for all the knowledge they have of all whales, but especially the orca." She rented Balcomb the floor for seventy-five dollars a month, and thus, by July of 1979, the Whale Museum was born. By 1989, the entire building belonged to the Museum.

The ghostly character of the old hall became apparent, some say, during the Whale Museum's extensive renovations in 1979. According to a 2007 article in the *Spokesman-Review*,

"In 1979, Noreene Ignelzi, who now lives in Newport, Ore., worked as a building supervisor when The Whale Museum was being built. She frequently slept upstairs in a loft area during the construction. One night she woke up and saw a tall man with dark hair standing in front of the door. The man she described could easily have been Straub. A current museum employee says that she has often felt a positive presence when she is in the building alone.

She likened this to a feeling of being watched over in a good way."

Though by all accounts Straub was red-haired, perhaps it was the shadows of the darkened hall that gave the specter its dubious coloration.

Various other odd occurrences have been reported at the Museum, as well—such as the dark, shadowy figures seen looming in the second-story windows, and the "phantom handprints," child-sized, that appear on the glass despite frequent cleaning. According to local legend, a group of island children had secretly observed the hanging from the hall's advantageous second floor; though the throngs of schoolchildren who annually visit the Museum may present a more likely explanation for the supposedly supernatural smudging.

Whatever the case may be, there can be no doubt that the old Whale Museum, ex-Odd Fellows Hall and ex-courthouse, has taken on a mantle of great importance in the town of Friday Harbor—spiritually or otherwise.

# Friday Harbor Laboratories

*On the north shore, and a little to the east of Friday Harbor, lies a level stretch of land which the early settlers called Channel Prairie. [...] Just here the first surveyors set aside a federal reserve, which in 1922 passed into the hands of the University of Washington. And here a new settlement is growing up; the home of one branch of the state university, known as the Biological station.*

*Most of the buildings are of the one-story cottage type, built of cement, hollow tile, plaster and roofing tile; and present a cheery appearance in their setting of evergreens. The woods are crowding closer each year, as if they recognized the fact that friends have settled near; so that now it would be hard to believe that this spot was once a prairie.*

*Here we find five laboratories, 24x56 feet; a larger two-story building with kitchen, dining room, library, etc. as well as several cottages for caretakers, faculty and their families. The students live in tents, as the classes are held in the summer. Those taking the course are mostly teachers, and other researchers who wish to make their summer work as much of a vacation as possible.*

*To this branch of a university, hidden away on the shore of an island, come doctors of all degrees from all over the world; and let's not forget that the word "doctor" is higher than professor. It's rather easy to "profess" something, but the title of doctor is won by "degrees."*

Such was early historian Sophie Walsh's description of the Friday Harbor Laboratories as they appeared in 1929—today, the site is a state-of-the-art center for the study of all things marine and biological. Decades before, the land had been home to Joe Friday, a Hawaiian ex-Hudson's Bay herder who had settled on the bay with his family in the 1850s. According to legend, a Royal Navy survey ship had visited the bay and sent a party ashore to ascertain its name. "Man" Friday, as he was sometimes known—a reference to the *Robinson Crusoe* character —was confused, and thought that the officer was asking for his name. His Hawaiian-language surname unintelligible to the Englishmen, the surveyors recorded the man's name as "Friday"—and the harbor was christened accordingly.

Later, the future University of Washington reserve became the final resting place of the infamous Richard Straub. Hanged for murder in 1897, Straub was subsequently buried in a remote plot on what was then known as Channel Prairie. Today, the grave's exact location is unknown—though it undoubtedly lies somewhere beneath the current campus.

The Friday Harbor Laboratories got their start in 1904, when Professors Trevor Kincaid and Thomas C. Frye of the University of Washington established the Puget Sound Marine Biological Station. The original location was on the south side of the harbor, in a cottage rented from San Juan pioneer Edward Warbass—the present-day site of Capron's Landing. The first year's enrollment, composed of nineteen students and two faculty members, built their own kitchen, laboratory, and dining tables, and spent their days wandering the reefs and shoals and muddy bays in search of specimens. By 1921, the university had managed to acquire the Point Caution Military Reservation, an undeveloped acreage on the north side of the harbor, and construction began on a new laboratory complex in 1923. The government, notably, retained the use of the land in case of wartime emergency.

In 1930, Professor Thomas G. "Tommy" Thompson took over directorship of the Biological Station from Professor Frye, following what many deemed a "largely-political confrontation." Thompson had recently secured an enormous grant from the Rockefeller Foundation to develop the oceanographic departents at both Friday Harbor and the Seattle campus, and renamed the station the "University of Washington

Oceanographic Laboratories." Frye, despite his founding role, would never set foot in the Labs again.

"Dr. Thompson was a chemist who specialized in sea water, a dynamic person who was bound to make the institution go places," said Professor Kincaid, years later. "Under him, the type of studies expanded and changed."

Under Thompson's leadership, the Labs gained a reputation as one of the premier research facilities on the West Coast, and as the only marine laboratory of its kind on the northeastern Pacific. "The work at Friday Harbor has broadened to such an extent that the labs have attracted foreign experts in their special marine fields and the station has been the scene of international conferences," wrote historian Lucile S. McDonald in 1961. "So much has been accomplished in studies of worldwide impact that the humble beginning of the place has been lost."

This important work was interrupted in 1942, when the government collected on its emergency caveat and the military reservation was reactivated. Director Thompson took a leave of absence to accept a Lieutenant Colonel's commission in the War Department, and the Coast Guard converted the laboratory buildings into barracks for a makeshift schoolhouse. An observation post was built for aircraft spotters, and a concrete gun emplacement was erected on a knoll overlooking the harbor. The Coast Guard would occupy the site until February of 1946.

After the war, the important work at the Labs

continued unabated. Princeton scientists Frank Johnson and Osamu Shimomura were fixtures at the station during their study of the bioluminescent crystal jellyfish, the proteins synthesized from which became a common marker of molecular activity; Shimomura was later awarded a Nobel Prize for his work. Later, beginning in the late 1970s, a number of ex-Soviet scientists would conduct research at the Labs—which had long since received their final name, the Friday Harbor Laboratories.

As is often the case, a surfeit of supernatural stories have surfaced concerning the site. One ghost hunter reported: "The Friday Harbor Labs have a dining hall that is haunted. Shadowy figures and other paranormal activity can be seen only out of the corner of one's eye. In the dining hall, the doors open and close by themselves and other creepy things happen."

"I can definitely vouch for that," says University of Washington alumni Justin McKeever. "Tons of weird stuff happens there that you never hear about. It's one hundred percent true what they say about the dining hall [...] I always got the weirdest feeling in there when I was in there alone. There's a pool table in there, and I was in there once, reading, I think, and I heard the sound of two pool balls hitting each other and rolling across the felt and dropping into a pocket. My old roommate in the dorms told me people would hear the piano in there, too, even when nobody was supposed to be in there, like at night [...] I don't know, some people think it's one of the Lab founders,

Professor [Frye], or other people were saying it was from a Native American burial ground."

Others are more unsure of the supposed spirit's identity, however. Some, such as island resident—and amateur psychic—Valerie Geyser, feel that presence may be that of the murderer Richard Straub. Geyser visited the Labs in the 1980s, when the grounds were fully open to the public, and says that she immediately sensed the ghostly energy.

"It's not what I would exactly call a *friendly* spirit," writes Geyser. "I felt an immense sort of negativity wash over me as I strolled through the campus [...] and although I didn't physically *see* an apparition, I could sense its anger and hatred towards the living. After all, imagine it; you're the spirit of a condemned man who's buried in an unmarked grave somewhere off in the middle of nowhere, and then a lot of highfalutin scientists come along and build a laboratory over you. You'd be angry, too!"

# *The Blair House*

The future Blair House was built in the early 1880s by
John H. Bowman, the first probate judge and auditor
of San Juan County. A Tennessean by birth, and previously an early homesteader on Orcas Island, Bowman
had arrived at Friday Harbor before the town was
built and soon recognized the area's great potential.
As auditor, his job was to sell county-owned lots to
prospective settlers and businessmen—and Bowman,
shrewdly, managed to cut a deal wherein he would
purchase the best of these lots, one hundred and fifty-
six-acres worth, for the measly sum of one hundred
and seventy-one dollars; to be paid off in increments,
taken from his fees accrued as county auditor. The
remaining lots were sold at similar rates to Joseph
Sweeney, a friend of Bowman's from his Orcas years.

Edward Warbass, who had selected the site as the county seat and effectively founded the town, was incensed; and declared that he would never again live in Friday Harbor.

Bowman's first house was on Spring Street, and still stands as the oldest residence in town. Later, he constructed a larger and more scenic home on Blair Avenue, which would become the Blair House Bed and Breakfast in later years. It was also owned for a time by Dr. Victor Capron, the Roche Harbor company doctor and a noted local politician. By 2007, it had been purchased by the nearby Spring Street School as a dormitory for off-island students, and in this iteration played host to a rather chilling tale, as related by a visitor named Kaitlyn* in 2005:

"I have only had one experience in the Blair House, but one I will not forget. It started simply when I was with my friend (I will call her Mimi) and we were walking up the stairs to the second story. You see, the Blair House is the oldest house in Friday Harbor, and it was a bed and breakfast until Spring Street School purchased it (or maybe they are renting it, I am not sure) as a dormitory in summer of 2007.

"Well, back to the story. I was also with my other friend (I'll call him Jimmy). Jimmy was in front of me and Mimi was behind and we were going upstairs. All of a sudden my heart beat a bit faster and I ignored myself, because sometimes my imagination goes a little wild. Then Mimi started crying randomly when we got to the top of the stairs. I later found out that she experienced what is known as a 'walk through.' This is when a ghost walks through you and you feel very mixed emotions; the emotions of the spirit.

"After that, Jimmy was standing by room #6 and I heard a knocking. I asked him why he knocked on the door, but he swore it came from inside the room! I do not know if he was trying to scare me or if he was telling the truth. I think he was just trying to creep Mimi and I out. Of course, upstairs, there are international students that live in the dormitories and one of them (who is Korean and no one can pronounce his name so we call him D.H.) had a key to one of the rooms. Unfortunately, it was not room 6, but room 4. Mimi, Jimmy, and I thought 'what the heck, we have nothing to lose, let's go ghost hunting,' so we went in the room without D.H. and sat in the closet in a circle holding hands (Mimi and I both have a slight 'sixth sense' and felt that the closet had a strong vibe). We asked if a ghost was present and if it was, to move something to prove its presence. Well, needless to say, nothing happened. So we left the room. But, as we left the room I noticed something different: the lampshade had been moved! I told Jimmy and Mimi and we got the heck out of there! We were very scared."

Kaitlyn later returned to the Blair House and reported a similar level of activity, this time measured with an array of ghost-hunting instruments:

"Mimi and I went back up to the Blair House to do some more ghost hunting. We were equipped with a tape recorder, a digital camera, a K2 meter, and my cell phone. Well, we went upstairs into room 6, which was an awkwardly built little room, but eventually ended up with no luck. Then we went into room 4 . . . and same thing! But, before we left I remembered that my cell phone had a recorder so we would try it once more. I asked 'what is your name?' to the spirit, and I got a delayed response, sounding like the name Richard when played at normal speed. So I slowed it down as I played it back to Mimi. In slo-mo it sounded like Corey or Charlie.

"Then, we left . . . well, leave it to Mimi to research the Blair House. And it turns out that there was a man who lived in the Blair House and his name was Charlie. He had a wife named Shirley. Charlie died of a heart attack. Mimi and I believe that we made contact with Charlie."

Today, the Blair House has been extensively remodeled, and is now the upscale and award-winning Friday Harbor Grand Bed and Breakfast—while paranormality of the type detailed above is not known to still occur. Perhaps the only element of the past to truly linger on at the old Bowman place is the legacy of double-dealing and chicanery which gave Friday Harbor its final form.

# The Courthouse

For years after the county's incorporation, the San Juan County courthouse had occupied a series of small, ramshackle buildings along Spring Street. By the fall of 1905, the last of these structures—the cramped courthouse that had been too small to house the Straub trial—was deemed unsafe for use in county affairs, and a petition was circulated to construct an edifice more befitting of the promising new municipality. The motion passed with a margin of ten-to-one, and construction commenced in the spring of 1906. The stately, red-brick courthouse was designed by Seattle architect William P. White in the Second Renaissance style, for a total cost of fourteen thousand dollars. The materials were all locally-produced, with brick from Orcas Island and lime from the local quarries.

By all appearances, it was shaping up to become a centerpiece for the burgeoning comm-unity—but serious issues would soon arise.

On October 18th, a subcontractor called the Franklin Fireproofing Company was concreting the roof when a twenty-by-thirty-foot section "gave way and carried the second floor, also reinforced concrete, with it, piling up a mass of timbers, wire and concrete on the main floor in the corner which is to be occupied by the auditor's office," according to the *San Juan Islander*. The only injury, fortunately, was sustained by county commissioner Michael S. Donohue, whose thumb was slashed open by a reinforcing wire. This collapse is likely what spawned the later rumors of a worker being "entombed" in wet concrete.

The issues continued. On a wintry evening in 1913, the citizens of Friday Harbor were awakened by a tremendous crash. A section of brick coping had collapsed, taking with it a good deal of the cornice-work—it seemed that water had seeped behind the lower firewall, due to shoddy masonry, and that the past decade's succession of freezing and thawing had warped the wall to such a degree that a toppling was inevitable.

"Brick masons say the work on the court house is a disgrace to their profession, and that this portion in particular was laid without any regard for rules of the trade, or workmanship. In other words the contractor who did the job 'worked' the county," declared the

*Islander.*

By the early 1980s, issues with the already-unstable courthouse had finally come to a head. While an addition was built to house the expanded county departments, the original 1906 structure was found to be severely unsound and likely to collapse in the event of an earthquake. The old courthouse was vacated in 1983, and the future of the historic building, deemed a "public nuisance," was now uncertain.

Thankfully, salvation arrived the following year, when a group of concerned citizens managed to secure a spot for the courthouse on the National Register of Historic Places. The group, called the Straights of Juan de Fuca, hoped to convert the storied structure into a community theater. This plan, however, never panned out. A special advisory ballot was passed in 1989 which allowed the old courthouse to be restored to its former use. The state allotted one hundred and forty-nine thousand dollars for the task, and the San Juan County Courthouse reopened with a ribbon-cutting ceremony in 1991.

Ever since, numerous reports have surfaced of ghostly activity at the old county seat—two ghosts, mainly, one for the old section and one for the new. In the original courthouse, a ghostly judge has been seen presiding over an empty court and wandering the halls in his flowing black robe. Some contend that the spirit is that of Judge John R. Winn, who sentenced Richard Straub to hang; others, that it is Judge George A. Joiner, who oversaw the similarly infamous Tom

Robertson murder trial of 1902. Regardless, this phantom judiciary has supposedly startled many a county employee over the years.

In the newer section of the courthouse, a similarly supernatural civil servant of a different type is said to haunt the halls. "Mary the Teacher," allegedly a hold-over from the old schoolhouse that once occupied the site, is often encountered in the upstairs women's restroom. Though the differing names would suggest otherwise, this spirit is supposedly that of turn-of-the-century schoolmarm Carrie M. Busby, who had once served as the county school superintendent, and, formerly, as a teacher at the since-demolished District No. 9 schoolhouse. She had lived across from the county seat in what is now known as the Busby House, which currently serves as the San Juan County Legislative Building—the old school site is now occupied by the courthouse parking lot. Today, cold spots are commonly reported, as are the sounds of stall doors slamming of their own accord.

Local ne'er-do-wells have supposedly experienced a host of ghostly activity while confined in the attached holding cells. The San Juan County Sheriff's Office maintains their headquarters in an annex of the courthouse, along with a small unit of holding cells for detainees awaiting trial or transport to the larger jail facilities off-island. One such inmate was Friday Harbor local Sean Kinzler*, whose experience in the courthouse cells in 2009 left him deeply unnerved.

"They picked me up for drunk and disorderly,"

laughs Kinzler. "Long story. We'll just say I got into it with a guy down at Herb's [a Friday Harbor tavern that burned in 2022]. Guys get way too comfortable running their mouth these days. [...] They could have nailed me for assault easily, but nobody pressed charges or anything, thank god. But they still picked me up and figured on throwing me in the drunk tank for the night. Problem was, it was Friday, and they don't have court until Monday. So me being a little rowdy on a Friday night turned into the longest weekend ever.

"It was just me in the cells. They got these little rooms in the Sheriff's Office that aren't really cells like you'd think of, with bars and stuff, but that's where they keep you until your court date, or until you go off-island if you're doing county time. So I was stuck in this little room that felt more like a psych ward, that just had a door with a window in it so the deputies could look in and make sure you weren't doing nothing crazy. No bueno, man. And they didn't do electronic home detaining like they do now, so I was stuck in there for the long haul. I figured I'd try to get some sleep, but I'm going to tell you, they really don't make it easy. They give you this thin little mattress that's hard as hell and it's vinyl, so it makes you feel like you're sleeping on a gym mat or something. But I was pretty tired, so eventually I dozed off.

"I woke up at probably two or three in the morning—I couldn't tell you for sure because there's no clocks in there—and I woke up because I was shivering like crazy. When I tell you it was cold in there, I mean it was freaking cold. Like, I was seeing my breath, and there was frost or whatever all over the window. I was so confused, because for one thing it was summer, or late spring, and it should not have been that cold. Then I realized the light in the hall was off. And it's *never* off, I mean that's like a policy for them—so obviously something was wrong. And then I look up and I see this face at the door, looking in at me through the window.

"I thought for a second that it was the jailer, but it wasn't. At all. It looked like a man's face, but totally white, like white as a sheet, and the eyes were totally black. I wanted to scream so bad, but I couldn't. It felt like all I could do is stare at this freaking thing! As I'm watching it, it's mouth opened, and it just kept opening and opening until it's jaw was unhinged, like a snake, and it was wider than any human or animal could possibly be. And then [...] I don't know how to describe it, but the light came on and I snapped out of it. I could move again, and it felt like I'd been underwater, running out of air, and I just came back to the surface. Something like that. Anyway, the guy or thing was gone, and I was so freaked out I jumped out of bed and started hammering on the window, yelling for the deputy. Finally he came over with a coffee mug in his hand and he looks at me like I'm the biggest r—d in the world. I told him what happened and I asked him why the lights went out, and he said the lights *hadn't* gone out. They'd been on the whole time, and he said he hadn't been asleep or anything, either. Who knows if that's true. But he had no idea what I was talking about, and he said nobody else had been in the office or he'd have known about it. I didn't sleep the rest of the time I was in there. I was falling asleep in court, it was so bad. But I was just glad to be out of that place. It was pure evil."

Kinzler is hesitant to speculate on just what it was he claimed to have seen that night—though he did mention rumors that an inmate had died in the holding cells under mysterious circumstances at some unknown date in the past. While such rumors are undoubtedly unfounded, tales of a terrifying entity at the Sheriff's Office at least serve to further deter troublemakers who would be loath to encounter such a thing themselves.

# The Denizen of the Deep

On neighboring Orcas Island, hushed talk of "sea monsters" stretched back to May of 1909, when loggers encountered a terrifying serpent-like creature in the waters off Terrill Beach. Such rumors were relatively unknown on San Juan—that is, until a wave of serpent sightings swept the area in 1933. Like the "phantom plane" craze of the First World War, the "flying disc" frenzy of 1947, and the sasquatch mania of '75, a torrent of sea monster run-ins were reported, mainly originating from Vancouver Island and British Columbia. The excitement grew so great that a Victoria newspaperman named Archie Wills christened the creature *Cadborosaurus*, in honor of its purported home of Cadboro Bay. The taxonym has endured, though today it is frequently shortened to simply

"Caddy."

Though the serpents seemed to be a mainly Canadian phenomenon, a few took place in the boundary waters between Vancouver and San Juan. In early October of 1933, a Victoria barrister and legislative clerk named Major W.H. Langley was taking his wife for a leisurely Sunday cruise across Haro Strait when something massive roiled up from the deep. As Major Langley described: "The time was about 1:30 p.m. [...] We were not talking and we were proceeding quite slowly and silently when suddenly my attention was attracted by a very loud and remarkable noise, something between a grunt and a snort, accompanied by a huge hiss."

The Major shouted for his wife to join him on-deck, and the couple watched as a monstrous creature "as big as the back of a large whale" breached the surface roughly one hundred feet off the port bow. This was no whale, however—for as Major Langley told the *Victoria Daily Times*, it was "entirely different in many respects." He continued:

"Its color was very distinct as the sun was shining brightly on its wetted surface and it was such a short distance away that there could be no mistaking it. Just shortly after it went down a swirl appeared on the surface of the water ahead of the *Dorothy* [Langley's sailboat]. My wife saw it break water a very short time afterwards on the other side of Fulford Reef. The appearance was exactly similar, but it was much further away and had travelled fast. The only part of it that we saw was a huge dome of what was apparently its back."

Major Langley added that he had been cruising about local waters for nearly forty years, and that he had once even accompanied a whaling expedition to Barkley Sound—in other words, he knew what a whale looked like, and the thing he'd seen on Haro Strait was no cetacean.

Another Victoria official, Provincial Archives clerk Fred Kemp, was surprised to hear of Langley's tale; as it turned out, Kemp and his family had witnessed something nearly identical the previous year. The Kemps had been spending an easygoing August day on diminutive Chatham Island, which commands a sweeping view of the strait, when Mrs. Kemp noticed a disturbance in the water. As the *Times* reported,

*When Mr. Kemp's attention was drawn to the monster, he stated it was clearly evident that it was some huge denizen of the deep unknown in gulf waters. As the party watched, the monster slid about ten feet of its head and body on to a rock and commenced to rub itself against the rough surface.*

*At this time Mr. Kemp judged it to be about 300 or 400 yards away and although he could not see it distinctly was able to view its entire length, which lay on the surface of the water. From where he stood he could plainly see its serrated back which, near the tail, resembled the cutting edge of a saw. After staying for two or three minutes the animal slid off the rock and went on its way down the channel, thrashing the water into a lather with its tail. The sun glistening on its body clearly showed its color to be a greenish brown.*

*Mr. Kemp described its head as being oval shaped, as he was not able to see any distinguishing features.*

Kemp further noted that, like Langley, he was a longtime mariner on the inland sea; and that such creatures had been whispered of for years by the old salts. By both accounts, the "denizen of the deep" was around eighty feet long and "as wide as an automobile."

Upon publication of the two men's tales, the *Times* was flooded with letters from numerous locals who had also seen the serpent on Haro Strait.

"I was passing through the tide rips off [Ten Mile Point] when I suddenly noticed what looked like a large colored buoy about 300 yards ahead," described yachtsman R.C. Ross. "My chart gave no buoy in that vicinity, so I went towards it to see if it were some buoy that had broken loose. I got to within 100 yards of it when to my astonishment it slowly sank. I went right over the spot where it had been, but there was no sign of anything."

Ross continued, "I mentioned this strange incident to my friends on arriving here, and we decided it was a mirage caused by the fog. Since then Major Langley's strange experience has been told, so now it is possible that my eyes did not deceive me, and that what I saw was the back of our unknown visitor."

Victoria druggist W.B. Grant had a far more

terrifying run-in, writing: "I was fishing one Sunday morning about ten years ago off the golf links point, which is at the southeast end of the Victoria Golf Club, when I decided to go into the seaweed to free my lines. About sixty yards off a huge head poked up and say, I just shivered for about ten minutes. I only saw its head above water. At first I thought it might be a walrus, but then I discovered it had no tusks and was altogether too large. I should estimate that the head was between two feet and thirty inches wide. It had two eyes in the front and had whiskers. In general appearance it was very shaggy and it was brownish in color.

"After a good look around the creature ducked its head and I became alarmed as to whether it would come closer to me or would head away. I was relieved when I saw it bob up a considerable distance away. It was heading in the direction of Chatham Island at quite a speed and there was a break in the water quite a piece from its head, which indicated that its tail was thrashing there. I have no proper idea of its length, as I only saw its head.

"When I went home I told my family about my experience and my wife offered the suggestion that it might have come from Japan. It was the year of the great Japanese earthquake [the Great Kanto Earthquake of 1923] and she thought that perhaps some unusual creature had been released by it and may have come here."

This would not be the only description of the

creature to conjure images of the latter-day "Godzilla." Fred Kemp, in response to local scientists who had theorized the serpent to be a monstrous conger eel, wrote: "My first feelings on viewing the creature were of being transferred to a prehistoric period when all sorts of hideous creatures abounded. When the thing shoved its head on the rock it did so with a little movement that was not fishlike, but rather more like the movement of a huge lizard, the serrated back also bearing out this opinion." Others had speculated that "Caddy" was indeed some unknown descendant of the primordial *diplodocus*—or perhaps even the dinosaur itself.

Afterward, *Cadborosaurus* sightings began to spread well outside the Haro Strait. Duck hunter Cyril Andrews reported that Caddy had devoured a downed goldeneye off Pender Island, while telegraph lineman R.M. Elliott recalled having seen it while stringing wire on a remote stretch of coastline near Port Renfrew in 1917. He claimed to have shot it in the neck with a .30-30 Winchester.

Sightings gradually fell off over the years, with a few notable exceptions; for example, on New Year's Day, 1944, the creature was spotted in Mosquito Pass, in the maze of bays and channels between Henry Island and the north end of San Juan. As the *Friday Harbor Journal* of January 20th reported, with characteristic droll:

*Residents on the northwest side of San Juan Island gaped,*

*wiped their eyes, and stared in unbelief one day not long ago, when they beheld a fearsome marine monster besporting itself in the waters of Mosquito Pass. Coming right after New Year season, a number of more convivial souls rushed into town to sign the pledge, but thought better of it, believing that perhaps the water they drank when celebrating the holidays might have disagreed with them and caused the hallucination.*

*The animal was described as anywhere up to 100 feet long, with a coiling body like a python and a head like a cow, horns and all. It had a forked tongue, fire was shooting from its eyes, and it was bellowing like the fog horn at the Lime Kiln Light station. Last seen it was disappearing behind the little island in the middle of the Pass.*

*Several days later it appeared again, and this time the natives really did think of swearing off their favorite beverage for good. There it was—believe it or not!—and on it came, snorting and kicking up a wake that almost caused a tidal wave along the Henry Island shore, from Pearl Island to Mitchell Bay. Once more it disappeared, and the watchers shook their heads and wondered.*

*For a while it was the nine-day wonder of the north end of the Island, and then the mystery was solved—It was later learned that a San Juan woman had sold her pet cow to a man on Henry Island, and bossy becoming homesick had swum across Mosquito Pass to come home. She was taken back to Henry Island, but a few days later she swam back home again, causing all the excitement and delirium tremens.*

A more realistic sighting came a few decades later. On August 30th, 1967, a "convoy" of serpents were supposedly seen in the waters off Saxe Point, south of Cadboro Bay—an adult and three apparent offspring. Two years later, just a few days after the thirty-sixth anniversary of Major Langley's sighting, one of the juvenile serpents was spotted "frolicking" around Cadboro Bay, just twenty feet offshore.

"I first saw him two weeks ago but I didn't say anything to anyone then. I thought people would think I was out of my tree!" said a witness named Joan Foster.

"The creature that romped, dived and swam along this morning was about five feet in length, a darkish green color, and had a round head that was lizard-like. When it dived it flipped its head completely out of the water," reported the *Times*, which also printed Foster's sketch of the serpent. Witnesses named the young serpent "Fidele."

In more recent years—and, uncommonly, in American waters—a local woman named Phyllis Harsh claimed to have rescued a two-foot-long "baby dinosaur" on little Johns Island, just north of San Juan.

"The baby had become beached and, using a tree branch, Mrs. Harsh lifted the animal back into the sea where it was able to make its way back into deeper water," says the British Columbia Scientific Cryptozoology Club, a *Cadborosaurus* research group. "Mrs. Harsh has also stated for the record that she found what appeared to be a 'dinosaur' skeleton beneath an eagle's nest also on Johns Island as well as having seen a full-size Caddy specimen in Johns Island Passage in

1990."

Some thirty years earlier, too, a Waldron Island resident had shared his own account in a letter to the *Friday Harbor Journal*. The resident, "J.B.," wrote that he had seen a "snake-like" creature swimming in a curious motion just off the beach.

"It swam in scallops," said J.B. "There were NO fins visible from head to tail. The look was very alert. It swam very fast. When it saw me it went under, lifted again soon. Then swam on around the point.

"Now I can completely believe that this slender snake-like fellow could just as well as not grow to twenty feet, if this was a youngling. I can, now, believe every tale I ever heard about sea serpents. For whatever this was, it was so much like a snake scalloping through the sea effortlessly that it could as easily have been a baby sea serpent as a rat fish or eel. Me, I'll say henceforth that I have seen the sea serpent."

A second letter in the following issue, from "B.C.", seemed to corroborate this wild story.

"Thanks for reassuring me on what I saw some twenty or thirty years ago along Waldron's shore," the letter began. "As I recall now, everyone said I had imbibed in too much Friday Harbor cheer on my weekly trip to our County seat."

B.C. and a friend named John Sepich had been returning from Friday Harbor when they spotted a twenty-foot serpent swimming in the same "scalloping" manner off Sandy Point. B.C. speculated that this creature might have been the parent of J.B.'s apparent juvenile.

"I have seen most everything that swims on Puget Sound but never before, nor since, have I seen such a creature," B.C. concluded. "I know that you had not imbibed of any cheer that would bring you an illusion of the sea serpent!"

Just what is the serpent that has terrorized Canadians—and the occasional American—for so many decades? Various theories have been put forth since the earliest sightings, ranging from a long-lived *diplodocus* to the prehistoric whale *zeuglodon*, while well-known researchers Drs. Paul LeBlond and Edward Bousfield posit that Caddy, or Fidele, is reptilian in nature. Perhaps the *Victoria Daily Times* said it best back in 1933: "Whatever the mammal may be—huge squid or plesiosaurus—it certainly has been seen in the Gulf, and its presence reminds us that there are still more things in heaven and earth—and the sea as well—that are not dreamed of in the little two-by-four philosophy of mankind."

# *Bibliography*

## BOOKS

- Bagley, Clarence B. *Indian Myths of the Northwest.* Seattle: Lowman and Hanford, 1930

- Ball, Durwood. *Army Regulars on the Western Frontier, 1848-1861.* Norman: University of Oklahoma Press, 2001

- Bailey, Jo and Carl Nyberg. *Gunkholing in the San Juans.* Seattle: Nor'westing Publishing, 1985

- Bailey-Cummings, Jo and Al Cummings. *San Juan: The Powder-Keg Island.* Friday Harbor: Beach Combers, Inc., 1987

- Bancroft, Hubert Howe. *The Works of Hubert Howe Bancroft: History of Washington, Idaho, and Montana, 1845-1889.* San Francisco: The History Company, 1890

- Bave, Emelia. *San Juan Saga: A Unique History of the San Juan Islands and the Pig War Told in Words and*

*Pictures from the Long-Running Historical Pageant.* Friday Harbor: Long House Printcrafters and Publishers, 1976

- Boswell, Sharon A. and Lorelea Hudson. *Heritage Resources Investigations at the Limekiln Preserve, San Juan Island, San Juan County, Washington.* Seattle: Northwest Archaeological Associates, Inc., 2001

- Burn, June. *100 Days in the San Juans: A 1946 Voyage Through the San Juan Islands.* Friday Harbor: Long House Printcrafters & Pub-lishers, 1983

- Burn, June. *Living High: An Unconventional Autob-iography.* Friday Harbor: Griffin Bay Bookstore, 1992

- Clark, Ella E. *Indian Legends of the Pacific Northwest.* Berkeley: University of California Press, 1953

- Coulter, C. Brewster. *The Pig War, And Other Experiences of William Peck, Soldier 1858-1862, U.S. Army Corps of Engineers: The Journal of William A. Peck Jr.* Medford, Oregon: Webb Research Group, 1993

- Crawford, Jack J. *Time Shadows & Tall Tales: San Juan Island in Earlier Years* Friday Harbor: Illumina Publishing, 2010

- Danner, Wilbert R. *Limestone Resources of Western Washington.* Olympia: Washington Department of Conservation, 1966

- Evans, Lynette and George Burley. *Roche Harbor: A Saga in the San Juans*. Everett, Washington: B&E Enterprises, 1972

- Faber, Jim. *Steamer's Wake*. Seattle: Enetai Press, 1985

- Gibbs, Jim. *Lighthouses of the Pacific*. West Chester, Pennsylvania: Schiffer Publishing, 1986

- Gibbs, Jim. *Shipwrecks of the Pacific Coast*. Portland: Binfords & Mort, 1962

- Gibbs, Jim and Joe Williamson. *Maritime Memories of Puget Sound*. West Chester, Pennsylvania: Schiffer Publishing, 1987

- Gough, Barry M. *The Royal Navy and the Northwest Coast of North America, 1810-1914: A Study of British Maritime Ascendancy*. Vancouver: University of British Columbia Press, 1971

- Guinn, James Miller. *A History of California and an Extended History of Its Southern Coast Counties also Containing Biographies of Well-Known Citizens of the Past and Present*. Los Angeles: Historic Record Company, 1907

- Halliday, William R. *Caves of Washington*. Olympia: Washington Department of Conservation, 1963

- Higgins, David Williams. *The Mystic Spring and Other Tales of Western Life*. Toronto: William Briggs, 1904

- Higgins, David Williams. *The Passing of a Race and More Tales of Western Life*. Toronto: William Briggs, 1905

- Hunt, Herbert and Floyd C. Kaylor. *Washington, West of the Cascades*. Seattle: S.J. Clarke Publishing Company, 1917

- Jackson, Terry, John Wade, and Wally Botsford. *Fishermen and Fisheries of the San Juan Islands: Those Were the Good Ole' Days*. Friday Harbor: 2011

- Keith, Gordon (ed.) *The James Francis Tulloch Diary, 1875-1910*. Portland: Binford and Mort, 1978

- Lautner, Nina. *Ghosts of America – Washington State*. Atlanta: Stratus-Pikpuk, Inc., 2016

- Link, Chris. *Roche Harbor Lime Kilns, San Juan County, Washington*. Seattle: Northwest Archaeo-logical Associates, Inc., 2004

- MacDonald, Margaret Read. *Ghost Stories from the Pacific Northwest*. Little Rock: August House Publ-ishers, Inc., 1995

- MacDonald, William John. *A Pioneer*. Victoria: University of Victory Press, 1914

- Mayne, Richard. *Four Years in British Columbia and Vancouver Island: An Account of Their Forests, Rivers, Coasts, Cold Fields, and Resources for Colonization*. London: John Murray, 1862

### BIBLIOGRAPHY

- McCabe, James O. *The San Juan Island Boundary Question.* Toronto: University of Toronto, 1964

- McDonald, Lucile Saunders. *Making History: The People Who Shaped the San Juan Islands.* Friday Harbor: Harbor Press, 1990

- Meany, Edmond S. *Origin of Washington Geographic Names.* Seattle: University of Washington Press, 1923

- Miller, David Hunter. *San Juan Archipelago: Study of the Joint Occupation of San Juan Island.* Bellows Falls, Vermont: Windham Press, 1943

- Morgan, C.T. *The San Juan Story.* Friday Harbor: San Juan Industries, 1966

- Murray, Keith. *The Pig War.* Tacoma: Wash-ington State Historical Society, 1968

- Newell, Gordon R. *Ships of the Inland Sea.* Portland: Binfords & Mort, 1951

- Newell, Gordon R. (ed.) *The H.W. McCurdy Marine History of the Pacific Northwest.* Seattle: Superior Publishing Company, 1966

- Pratt, Boyd C. *Lime: Quarrying and Lime-making in the San Juan Islands.* Friday Harbor: Mulno Cove Publications, 2016

- Reigel, Joseph W. *Unusual Orcas Island: Ghost Stories and Other Legends from the Gem of the San Juans.* Eastsound: Orcas Island History Press, 2024

- Reigel, Joseph W. *Shipwrecks of the San Juans: A History of Maritime Disaster in the San Juan Islands.* Eastsound: Orcas Island History Press, 2024

- Richardson, David. *Magic Islands: A Treasure-Trove of San Juan Islands Lore.* Eastsound: Orcas Publishing Company, 1995

- Richardson, David. *Pig War Islands.* Eastsound: Orcas Publishing Company, 1990

- Roe, JoAnn. *The San Juan Islands: Into the 21st Century.* Caldwell, Idaho: Caxton Press, 2011

- Schwantes, Carlos A. *The Pacific Northwest: An Interpretive History.* Lincoln: University of Nebraska Press, 1989

- Shiels, Archie W. *San Juan Islands: The Cronstadt of the Pacific.* Juneau: Empire Publishing, 1938

- Simpson, Peter (ed.) *City of Dreams: A Guide to Port Townsend.* Port Townsend: Bay Press, 1986

- Stein, Julie K. *Exploring Coast Salish Prehistory: The Archaeology of San Juan Island.* Seattle: University of Washington Press, 2000.

- Stern, Bernhard J. *The Lummi Indians of Northwest Washington.* New York: Columbia University Press, 1934

- Strickland, Ron. *Whistlepunks and Geoducks: Oral Histories from the Pacific Northwest.* Corvallis: Oregon State University Press, 1990

- Suttles, Wayne. *The Economic Life of the Coast Salish of Haro and Rosario Straits.* New York: Garland Publishing, 1974

- Tarte, Neil. *The Building of Roche Harbor Resort by the Tarte Family.* Friday Harbor: Illumina Publishing, 2010

- *The San Juan Islands: Illustrated Supplement to the San Juan Islander.* Friday Harbor: 1901

- Thompson, Erwin. *Historic Resource Study, San Juan Island National Historical Park.* Denver: National Park Service, 1972

- *Told by the Pioneers: Tales of Frontier Life As Told by Those Who Remember the Days of the Territory and Early Statehood of Washington.* (3 vols). Olympia: Washington Pioneer Project, 1937-1938

- Vosper, Lloyd. *Cruising Puget Sound and Adjacent Waters.* Seattle: Westward Press, 1947

- Vouri, Mike. *Outpost of Empire: The Royal Marines and the Joint Occupation of San Juan Island.* Seattle: Northwest Interpretive Association, 2004

- Vouri, Michael. *The Pig War: Standoff on Griffin Bay.* Friday Harbor: Griffin Bay Bookstore, 1999.

- Wagner, Henry R. *Spanish Explorations in the Strait of Juan de Fuca.* Santa Ana, California: Fine Arts Press, 1933

- Walker, Richard. *Roche Harbor.* Charleston, South Carolina: Arcadia Publishing, 2009

- Walsh, Sophie. *History and Romance of the San Juan Islands.* Anacortes: Anacortes American Press, 1932

- Wray, Jacilee. *The Salmon Bank: An Ethnohistorical Compilation.* National Park Service, 2003

- Wright, E.W., ed. *Lewis & Dryden's Marine History of the Pacific Northwest.* Portland: Lewis & Dryden Printing Company, 1895

# ARTICLES

- Anderson, Ilene. "Why is Adah Beany's ghost haunting the room?" *Journal of the San Juans*, October 8, 1986

- "A Raid Upon Japs." *San Juan Islander*, January 24, 1901

- Bagby, Cali. "High heels, a hanging, and the Cry Baby House." *Islands Sounder*, October 30, 2012

- Bailey, Jo. "The Rest of the Story in the Roche Harbor Tragedy." *Islands' Sounder*, January 16, 1985

- Barry, J. Neilson. "San Juan Island in the Civil War." *Washington Historical Quarterly*, Vol. 19, 1928

- Bauer, Wolf. "Roche Harbor During the Recovering Thirties." *Journal of the San Juan Islands,* January 8, 2003

- Bellaine, Wesley Charles. "Personalities in the Military Occupation of San Juan Island." *Reserve Officer*, September, 1938

- Berman, William. "British and Indian Artifacts are Unearthed at English Camp." *Friday Harbor Journal*, July 16, 1970

- "Blakely Murder." *Anacortes American*, September 5, 1895

- Box, Dennis. "UFO sighting on San Juan." *Islands' Weekly*, February 16, 2015

- "Cadborosaurus Is Sighted Again By Island Residents." *Victoria Daily Times*, October 17, 1933

- "Caddy's Kiddy Spotted in Cadboro Bay?" *Victoria Daily Times*, October 8, 1969

- Carlson, Ann. "Pig War comes alive at English Camp ceremony." *Islands' Sounder*, August 19, 1998

- "Court House Damaged." *San Juan Islander*, January 17, 1913

- "Court House Roof Collapses." *San Juan Islander*, October 20, 1906

- "Day by Day Report of Operation Sea Wall." *Friday Harbor Journal*, September 21, 1961

- "Death of Mrs. R.H. Straub." *The Islander*, May 23, 1895

- "Defendant Straub." *The Islander*, October 17, 1895

- "Deputies study murder-suicide." *Bellingham Herald*, April 3, 1987

- DiFazio, Angelina. "Ghostly goings-on at Hotel de Haro." *Journal of the San Juans,* December 30, 1998

- "Disappearance of L. McKay is Mystery." *Friday Harbor Journal*, July 18, 1940

- Dodson, Lt. Cmdr. Kenneth (ret.) "Exercise Sea Wall." *Professional Notes, Notebook, and Progress*. U.S. Naval Institute, May, 1962

- "Double murder, suicide jolts San Juan." *Islands' Sounder*, April 8, 1987

- Dustrude, Tim. "Cry Baby House." *San Juan Island Update*, October 2, 2019

- Erickson, Eric. "Skeletons Identity Still Unknown." *Friday Harbor Journal*, February 1, 1962

- "Flying Saucers Old Stuff Here." *Friday Harbor Journal*, December 1, 1966

- "Found Guilty." *The Islander*, October 24, 1895

- "From Barren Rock to Lime." *Wilhelm's Mag-azine-The Coast*, September 1903

- Gainor, Chris. "Now It's Sasquatch vs. the Indians." *Vancouver Sun*, November 12, 1975

- Garrett, Anita Melanie. "Ghost of Cady Mountain." *Journal of the San Juan Islands*, October 25, 1978

- "Ghosts Gone." *San Juan Journal*, November 7, 1974

- Grant, David, Colt Denfeld, and Randall Schalk. "U.S. Navy Shipwrecks and Submerged Naval Aircraft in Washington: An Overview." Olympia: Office of Archaeology and Historic Preservation, 1996

- "Hanging of Kanaka Joe." *Puget Sound Dispatch*, March 12, 1874

- "Hatchet Buried by British and Americans at Historic English Camp on San Juan." *Bellingham Herald*, July 7, 1919

- "His Day of Doom is Fixed." *Seattle Post-Intelligencer*, February 19, 1897

- "Island Civilians May View Operation Sea Wall." *Friday Harbor Journal*, August 17, 1961

- "It's Quiet Now On Island After Troops End Test." *Bellingham Herald*, September 19, 1961

- "John S. McMillin Charged With Fraud." *San Juan Islander*, June 9, 1906

- Keppel, Bruce. "Aggressor Force Digs Into San Juan Island." *Bellingham Herald*, September 14, 1961

- Keppel, Bruce. "Sea Wall Troops Battle On." *Bellingham Herald*, September 17, 1961

- Koue, A. Lewis and Erwin N. Thompson. "English Camp: San Juan Island NHP Historic Structures Report - Part I." Olympia: Office of Archaeology & Historic Preservation, 1969

- Larson, Heather. "Hauntingly familiar." *Spokesman-Review*, October 28, 2007

- Larson, Nancy. "San Juan County Courthouse, 100 Years." *Journal of the San Juans*, Dec-ember 13, 2006

- Leeming, Frank III. "Three dead in family dispute." *Journal of the San Juans*, April 8, 1987

- "Letter to the Editor." *Friday Harbor Journal*, December 7, 1961

- "Letter to the Editor." *Friday Harbor Journal*, December 15, 1961

- Maddox, Dawn. "A Survey of Fraternal Halls and Public Meeting Places on San Juan, Orcas, Shaw, and Lopez Islands, San Juan County, Washington." Olympia: Office of Archaeology and Historic Preservation, 1980

- McDonald, Lucile S. "Curiosities on Rugged Blakely Island." *Seattle Times*, August 13, 1961

- McDonald, Lucile. "San Juan Limestone Resources." *Seattle Times*, September 13, 1959

- McDonald, Lucile Saunders. "The San Juan Limestone Trade." *Sea Chest*, March, 1983

- McKay, Charles. "History of San Juan Island." *Washington Historical Quarterly*, July, 1908.

- "McMillin Wins the Cowell Case." *San Juan Islander*, June 27, 1908

- "Men Guilty of Stealing Pig." *Friday Harbor Journal*, November 24, 1938

- "More People Tell of Seeing Serpent in Sea Near Here." *Victoria Daily Times*, October 6, 1933

- "Murder at San Juan." *Washington Standard*, May 24, 1873

- O'Ragan, Barney. "San Juan Correspondence." *Puget Sound Dispatch*, December 5, 1872

- "Our Sea Serpent." *Victoria Daily Times*, October 7, 1933

- " 'Pig War' Skeleton Found By Young Hunters." *Friday Harbor Journal*, January 25, 1962

- "Pot of Gold Discovered In Old Pig War Barracks." *Bellingham Herald*, July 20, 1970

- Pranger, Matt. "Boat and controversy sink off Stuart." *Journal of the San Juans*, December 11, 1991

# BIBLIOGRAPHY

- Pranger, Matt. "Sinking boat towed out of Roche." *Journal of the San Juans*, December 4, 1991

- Rasmus, S. Michelle. "Repatriating Words: Local Knowledge in a Global Context." *American Indian Quarterly*, Vol. 26, No. 2, Spring, 2002

- "Relive 1860s at English Camp." *Bellingham Herald*, August 21, 2002

- Robinson, Kathryn. "Seattle Spirits." *Seattle Weekly*, October 28, 1987

- Romines, Pat. "The Roche Harbor ghost – fact or fiction?" *Journal of the San Juan Islands*, March 29, 1995

- Roth, John. "Did ghost ship cut Opalco's cable?" *Journal of the San Juans*, June 10, 1992

- "San Juan Island shootings leave girlfriend, men dead." *Bellingham Herald*, January 12, 1985

- "San Juan Island Is Target of Three-Pronged Assault." *Bellingham Herald*, July 20, 1961

- "Saved from the Mob." *Seattle Post-Intelligencer*, September 5, 1895

- Schroeder, Tom. "Rediscovering a Coastal Prairie Near Friday Harbor." *Pacific Northwest Quarterly*, Vol. 98, No. 2, Spring 2007, pp. 55-63

- "Sea Serpent Season Is With Us Again." *Friday Harbor Journal*, January 20, 1944

- Shimizu, Cho, Kris Day Vincent and Lori Matsukawa. "The Japanese of Roche Harbor." San Juan Historical Museum Newsletter, Fall 2005

- "Skeleton Found on Island May Solve Old Mystery." *Bellingham Herald*, October 23, 1955

- "Skeleton is Found on Kady Mountain." *Friday Harbor Journal*, October 27, 1955

- "Slayings followed threats, friends say." *Daily Herald*, January 13, 1985

- Smith, Albert Goldwin. "Notes on the Problem of San Juan." *Pacific Northwest Quarterly*, April, 1940

- Stensland, Jessie. "Navy mum on whether Growler pilots saw UFOs." *Whidbey News-Times*, May 31, 2019

- "Strange Meteor Seen." *Friday Harbor Journal*, February 22, 1934

- "Straub Did Not Waver." *Seattle Post-Intelligencer*, April 24, 1897

- "Straub Found Guilty." *Seattle Post-Intelligencer*, October 21, 1895

- "Straub Gets One Month's Respite." *The Islander*, March 18, 1897

- "Straub Murder Trial: Irving Parberry the Chief Witness for the State." *Seattle Post-Intelligencer*, October 16, 1895, September 8, 1895

- "The Attempt to Lynch Straub." *Seattle Post-Intelligencer*, September 7, 1895

- "The San Juan Murder." *Puget Sound Dispatch*, June 12, 1873

- "The San Juan Murders." *Puget Sound Dispatch*, June 5, 1873

- "The San Juan Murder." *Washington Standard*, June 26, 1869

- "The Shocking Murder on San Juan Island." *Puget Sound Dispatch*, May 22, 1873

- "The Straub Murder Trial." *Seattle Post-Intelligencer*, October 5, 1895

- Thomas, Jean. "Island Hopping." *Journal of the San Juans*, November 28, 1974

- "Too Bad, Fellows, San Juan Sue Is Really Mrs." *Bellingham Herald*, September 18, 1961

- "UFO Sighted At Cannery Beach." *Journal of the San Juans*, July 26, 1977

- Van Alstyne, Richard W. "International Rivalries in the Pacific Northwest." *Oregon Historical Quarterly*, 1945

- "Villainous Murder." *The Islander*, September 5, 1895

- Vouri, Mike. "Scofflaws and Moonshine: San Juan's Stormy Joint Occupation." *San Juan Islander*, December 8, 2022

- Walsh, Sophie. "Heard at Friday Harbor." *Anacortes American*, October 24, 1929

- Walters, Bob E. "Cruisin' Time in the 1940s and '50s." *San Juan Islands Almanac, Vol. 9*. Friday Harbor: Long House Printcrafters and Publishers, 1983

- "Widespread Search for Cadborosaurus." *Victoria Daily Times*, October 19, 1933

- Woodbury, Chuck. "How One Pig Could Have Changed American History." *Out West,* No. 15, July, 1991

- "Yachtsmen Tell of Huge Sea Serpent Seen Off Victoria." *Victoria Daily Times*, October 5, 1933

# Index

www.ingramcontent.com/pod-product-compliance
Lightning Source LLC
Chambersburg PA
CBHW071719120626
46550CB00001B/298